# You're FLYING ME CRAZY!

## 101 Discourteous, Inconsiderate, Thoughtless, and Annoying Flying Situations

### John Reinhardt

# You're Flying Me Crazy!

USA edition

ISBN: 979-8-9876310-7-2 (Paperback)
ISBN: 979-8-9876310-8-9 (eBook)

For information contact:

John Reinhardt
802-236-4147
youredrivingmecrazy.com

Cover illustration by Malane Newman
Cover and text design by John Reinhardt Book Design

## Important Notes

Please refer to the FAA and TSA websites for rules and regulations. This book focuses primarily on inappropriate and discourteous flying behaviors/ situations and how to avoid them.

**Printed in the United States of America**

To my wife, Lynn,
and our daughter, Kim

# Acknowledgments

First of all, thank you to all the pilots, attendants, and employees of all airlines who work hard to make our flying experience safe, enjoyable and efficient.

Thank you to my wife, Lynn, for everything.

Thank you to our daughter, Kim, for her exceptional insight and contributions on the many of the topics in this book.

Thank you to Beth Hollen (retired airline flight attendant) for her invaluable insight, experience, and assistance.

Thank you to Malane Newman. Her incredible illustration skills are showcased on this book's cover.

And finally, thank you to all the people out there who are NOT flying me crazy!

# Contents

CONTENTS

CONTENTS

# CONTENTS

# CONTENTS

# Introduction

Growing up, my dad owned a small airplane, and some of my best teenage memories were spent in the sky with him. Saturdays meant taking off for no particular reason other than the joy of flying—hopping from one small airport to another, grabbing lunch in a neighboring state, and returning home to wash and clean the plane together. He even taught me how to fly, though I never went on to get my license. Maybe that was for the best.

Commercial flying, of course, is a very different experience. The process alone can test anyone's patience, but add in the inconsiderate, oblivious, and downright rude behaviors of fellow passengers, and suddenly the journey feels less like travel and more like a carnival of aggravation.

As someone who studies human and social behavior, airports and airplanes have become an endless parade of fascinating—and often frustrating—examples of how people act when they're stressed, rushed, or simply unaware of those around them. Over the years, I've observed more than a hundred behaviors that range from mildly annoying to shockingly disrespectful, and it seems the trend is only getting worse.

Still, my deepest respect goes to the pilots, flight crews, and airline employees who manage to navigate not only the skies but also the unpredictable behaviors of the traveling public. This book is dedicated to them—and to anyone who has ever found themselves wondering, somewhere between boarding and baggage claim, "What on earth is happening to people these days?"

**Let's go flying!**

# Develop Good Flying Habits

Flying isn't what it used to be. Less legroom. Longer lines. smaller seats, Security theater. These days, air travel tests your patience, posture, and politeness.

Before we dive into the bad habits and maddening moments, let's start with the good ones.

Every flyer should know and understand FAA and TSA rules and regulations. We hope others will follow them, but they often don't. Prepare for the worst while modeling the best.

This book will help you:

- Spot irritating, disrespectful, and inconsiderate behaviors
- Defuse tension before it escalates
- Fly smarter, act better, and avoid being "that person"

With the right mindset and a few clever strategies, you can enjoy your flight, anticipate problems, and create options. Knowing what might go wrong reduces stress—and makes you the kind of passenger others hope to sit beside.

Let's make flying better—for ourselves and everyone around us

**Let's do the right thing!**

# Challenge

As you read through the book, note how many of these topics you see flyers do, including yourself, by marking the check boxes before each topic on the Contents page.

After you've read the book, and you know what to look for, take the book with you on your flight and challenge your friends to see who can spot the most situations mentioned in this book.

Feel free to let me know how many you've seen. There are a lot of them, so I doubt you'll see them all anytime soon. But given the fact that we are talking about millions of people flying every day, you might!

Also, if you see any bad habits or situations not mentioned in this book, let me know by emailing me at designerofbooks@gmail.com. I'll make note of them and possibly include them in the next edition and give you credit.

Be sure to check out my other "Crazy!" books at YoureDrivingMeCrazy.com.

**Buckle up!**

# Babies and Children

**Whaaaa!** We've all been there. The wail. The whimper. The full-throttle meltdown at 30,000 feet. Flying with children is not only a challenge for the parents, but for the passengers and the flight attendants (who deserve hazard pay and a medal).

Most parents come prepared with snacks, toys, pacifiers, and prayers. They do their best to keep their little ones quiet and civilized. But then there are the others—the ones who are unaware their baby's scream is now the soundtrack of our flight.

Flying is supposed to be a quiet time. A nap. A movie. Maybe a Bloody Mary. But when you're seated next to a non-stop crying baby, all that goes out the window. You try to be understanding. But after the third hour of "Whaaaa!" you start fantasizing about parachutes.

I've flown with infants. It can be fun. It can be a disaster. Our daughter got sick on her first flight. That was definitely not fun. And there's little you can do but hope you are capable of calming your child—or at least apologizing with chocolate.

Earplugs help. Noise-canceling headphones are a godsend. Flight attendants do their best, but they're not miracle workers. This is just one of those facts of life in the friendly skies.

So, if you bring your baby on board, please do your best to keep them quiet. And if that fails, small treats for your seat neighbors go a long way toward forgiveness.

Maybe we need a sign at the plane's entrance: "Baby on Board—Brace Yourself!"

## Going Through Security

**Oh yeah, this is going to be fun!** Since 9/11, airport security has become a full-contact sport. When airports reopened after that fateful day, the screening process was intense—a slow-motion obstacle course of belts, bins, and body scans. And rightly so.

You're up against long lines that snake like a theme park ride (minus the fun), multiple stations where you shed layers like a molting bird, and the dreaded hat-and-belt removal that makes you feel like you're undressing for a very uninterested audience.

The entire process moves at a glacial pace, and if your bag contains anything remotely mysterious, you'll be pulled aside for the full unpack-and-pat-down experience. And yes, sweat can trigger the alarm. So, try not to stress. (Good luck with that.)

One minute you're breezing through, the next you're in a glass box doing the Hokie Pokie. The area is crowded, noisy, and charged with the tension of "Will I be the chosen one?" If you are, you might miss your flight and end up in the waiting area, eating overpriced chips and contemplating your life choices.

Avoidable rookie mistakes include forgetting about the 8-ounce water bottle, pepper spray, or—heaven forbid—a pocket knife. Wearing too many layers can also trigger the scanner's fashion police mode. And if your laptop is buried like pirate treasure, you'll be holding up the line while everyone behind you silently curses your packing strategy.

Want to skip the drama? Apply for TSA PreCheck. It's like the VIP lounge of security—shoes stay on, laptops stay put, and your dignity remains intact.

Bottom line: be prepared. Empty your pockets, ditch the belt, and channel your inner Zen master. Airport security can be a challenge, but with a little foresight (and a lot of patience), you'll make it through with your sanity—and snacks—intact.

Next!

# Wrong Seat

**Am I supposed to sit on your lap?** You board the plane, ticket in hand, eyes scanning for your seat number. You spot it—or so you think—only to find someone already parked there, headphones on, tray table down, living their best airborne life. You double-check your boarding pass. Yep, that's your seat. So, what now? Sit on their lap?

Welcome to the modern aviation ritual known as The Seat-Switch Standoff—a passive-aggressive ballet of confusion, denial, and territorial squatting. It's surprisingly common. People misread seat numbers (14C vs. 41C), rely on glitchy apps, or simply decide they prefer your window seat. Some even argue that seat numbers are more of a suggestion than a rule.

If you find yourself in this awkward tango, start by confirming your seat. Then, politely inform the person (with a smile, if you can) of their mistake. If they resist, don't escalate. Summon the flight attendant. They wield the power and authority of the sky. Let them do the heavy lifting.

Of course, if your seatmate starts the flight with a territorial dispute, odds are they won't be swapping snacks or sharing travel tips. You may be in for a long, silent flight punctuated by passive-aggressive elbow wars.

# Rolling Carry-Ons In the Aisle

**Bang, bump, nudge.** If I wanted to spend half an hour being assaulted by rogue luggage, I'd sign up for a professional pillow fight. At least there, the bruises come with a trophy.

I usually book an aisle seat. It's strategic—easy access to the restroom, a chance to stretch, and a quick exit when the wheels touch down. But this prime real estate comes with a price: the carry-on gauntlet.

Here they come—travelers dragging bags like they're walking untrained Labradors. The wheels wobble, the handles sway, and inevitably—whack!—my elbow becomes collateral damage.

If I'm lucky, I get a sheepish grin. If not, I get a bruised knee and a new reason to write this book.

To the aisle marauders: your bag does not have a "mind of its own." You do. So, use it. Roll the bag in front of you, not beside you. Keep it in the aisle, not in my personal space. And if you've packed more than you can manage, maybe—just maybe—it's time to reevaluate your relationship with overhead bins.

# Backpacks

**Did you just hit my backpack with your head?**
Aisle seats definitively have advantages—easy exit, quick access, and a little leg stretch. But beware, though, the backpacks are coming for you.

As passengers shuffle like sheep down the narrow airplane aisle, backpacks become battering rams. People twist and turn like confused ballet dancers, unaware that their shoulder-mounted cargo is smacking heads, knocking drinks, and invading personal space. And when they do finally reach their row? Off comes the backpack with a dramatic fling—no glance, no warning— just a surprise thwack to the nearest skull.

I get it, airplane cabins are tight. There's barely room for us, let alone a backpack strapped to your back like a medieval shield. So, here's a radical idea: take it off. Carry it in front of you. Slide it over your rolling bag handle. Make one manageable unit. It's not just courteous—it's survival.

And once you're seated, remember the backpack goes *under* the seat. That overhead bin is reserved for the rolling carry-ons that physically can't fit below.

Because if you don't care...well then, let's get ready to rumble.

# Flirting

**Do you come here often?** The plane is not a cocktail lounge—it's a pressurized aluminum tube hurtling through the sky with 200 strangers and one shared armrest.

There's a certain breed of traveler who believes they're the in-flight entertainment. Whether it's a bar, a beach, or boarding group B, they strut through life convinced they're the main character in everyone's romance comedy. They're not.

On a plane, personal space is already a myth. Add unsolicited compliments, lingering glances, and the occasional "accidental" arm graze, and suddenly your aisle seat feels like a trap. Unless, of course, you're into that sort of thing. In which case—carry on, Casanova.

And let's not forget the flight attendants, who somehow manage to serve drinks, soothe crying babies, and deflect creepy comments all while balancing a tray of snacks. They're not your therapist, your matchmaker, or your fantasy. They're professionals. Respect them.

Flying is not an airborne dating app. If you must shoot your shot, try the airport bar—at least there, the exits aren't blocked by beverage carts. Or better yet, charter a private jet and flirt with your reflection.

# Overly Affectionate Couples

**Get a room!** There's always one. That couple who treats row twenty-seven like a honeymoon suite. Maybe it's the altitude, maybe it's the recycled air, maybe it's the multiple drinks before the flight, but something about being 30,000 feet in the air makes them think PDA stands for "Public Display (on an) Airplane."

Now, don't get me wrong. It's wonderful they adore each other. Holding hands, sharing a sweet kiss, whispering sweet nothings. But when the sweet nothings turn into full-blown somethings, and the armrest becomes a wrestling mat, it's time to call a timeout.

We're all trapped in this flying sardine can together. Your seatmates didn't sign up for a live show (or maybe they did!). And the aisle isn't a runway for romance—it's for flinging backpacks, beverage carts, and bathroom breaks.

So, here's a friendly reminder: if your love can't wait, maybe book a private jet. Or better yet, wait until you reach your destination.

Trust me, turbulence isn't the only thing that makes people queasy.

# The Mile-High Club

**Are you a member of the Mile-High Club?** Well then—congratulations, I suppose. It's not exactly an easy feat. Some consider it a badge of honor; a daring accomplishment whispered about in the aisles like urban legend. But honestly, it's more frat party than fantasy.

Flight attendants, bless them, have enough to deal with. Now they're referees in the sky, trying to prevent amorous acrobatics in a space barely big enough to turn around. These attempts clog up the restroom, generate suspicious noises, and leave the place looking like a dorm room after homecoming. Not ideal.

Sure, some thrill-seekers are drawn to the risk, the adrenaline, the "we did it!" brag. But for the sake of everyone else onboard—those just trying to survive the pretzel snack and the seatbelt sign—maybe hold off until you reach your destination. Surely you can "keep it together" for a few hours.

This isn't good. It's not glamorous. It's just gross.

## Snoring

**Z-z-z-z-z-z!** If only the snorer could hear themselves and be as annoyed as the rest of us.

What are your options? Keep nudging them like a passive-aggressive woodpecker? Or shift around in your seat with theatrical flair, hoping your "accidental" elbow lands just right?

Flight attendants? They're busy keeping the plane in the sky, serving drinks, and maintaining peace among 200 strangers. Waking snorers isn't in the manual.

Sometimes, a well-timed throat clear—just loud enough to jolt the snorer back to silence. But beware: karma flies . You might be the one snoring next time.

Best bet? Crank up your headphones, zone out, and let the airborne symphony of nasal turbulence fade into the background.

## Setting Fan to Hit Others

**Is there a window open?** Nope—just someone cranking their overhead fan like it's a leaf blower.

The cabin heats up fast during boarding, so once I'm buckled in, I aim that little nozzle to cool my forehead. But while some of us run warm, others are bundled up like it's a polar expedition. That's why I always make sure the airflow hits me—not my unsuspecting neighbors.

Some folks, however, seem to think they're installing central air for the entire row. Their fan is so strong it could dry laundry.

Now, if you're in the dreaded middle seat, you've got prime access to the fans. Want to earn both armrests and eternal gratitude? Offer to adjust the airflow to your seatmates' liking.

Being aware of others used to be common sense. Now it's practically a superpower. So, before takeoff, do your part: aim the breeze at your own dome and leave your neighbors in peace.

# Noisy Eating

**Crunch, crunch, crunch...** Oh boy. If you think a crying baby is bad, try sitting next to a loud chewer.

And why do they always end up next to me with a bottomless snack bag? It's like they're on a personal mission to sample every crunchy item in the sky.

There's not much you can do except crank up your earbuds and pray for turbulence. And whatever you do, don't look at them. They don't know. They think they're being normal.

And why do airplanes hand out the noisiest snacks imaginable? Pretzels, crackers, granola bars—each one louder than the last.

Meanwhile, I'm sitting there, teeth clenched, inner voice screaming, "Stop it!" while they blissfully munch through mile-high mayhem.

# Farting

**Rrrrrriiiiiiip!** Yep. It's that unmistakable sound— the trumpet of doom. Just like those who chew like barnyard animals or snore like chainsaws, the farter rarely hears or smells their own offense. Meanwhile, the rest of us are left gasping for mercy.

There's almost nothing worse than sitting next to someone who lets one go. And the "silent but deadly" variety? They're the ninjas of nasal assault— no warning, no honor, just pure devastation.

What can you do? Not much. You can't un-smell it. You can't un-sit next to it. You can only pray for a breeze or a sudden urge to check your phone in another room.

So, here's a plea to all you stealth bombers out there: if you feel the rumble, take it to the bathroom. That's what it's for.

Because in the end, it's not just about gas—it's about class.

# Bags Too Heavy

**What have you got in here, gold bricks?** You're running late. You round the corner to baggage check-in and—bam!—a line longer than a TSA agent's lunch break. You breathe. You wait. You inch forward. Almost there...

But no. The couple in front of you has over-weight bags. Not just a little over—Olympic deadlift over. So, begins the great airport shuffle: unzip, reshuffle, rezip, repeat. One bag into another. Shoes into carry-ons. Toiletries into purses. A winter coat wrapped around a beach hat. It's a Cirque du Soleil act of poor planning.

Is it too much to ask to weigh your bags before you leave home?

You have a scale. You probably weigh yourself daily. So, weigh your bag! Or better yet, buy a $10 luggage scale. Some bags now come with built-in scales. There's no excuse for turning the check-in line into a yard sale.

And while we're on the topic of mass and gravity, why do some carry-ons weigh more than a small child? If you can't lift it into the overhead bin without a spotter, it's not a carry-on. Check it.

Also, can someone explain this math to me?

A 400-pound person with a 50-pound checked bag, a 40-pound carry-on, a 25-pound backpack, and a 5-pound bag of chicken nuggets boards without issue. But my 51-pound suitcase? That'll be $100, please.

If weight is so critical, why does it only matter when it's in my checked bag?

Let's put a stop to the weight wait. Weigh your bags. Pack like a grown-up. And if you're over the limit, step aside and let the rest of us fly.

## Yelling at Employees

**Oh yeah? Well, you're an idiot!** We've all seen a passenger, red-faced, puffed up like a balloon animal gone wrong, unleashing a verbal tirade on an unsuspecting airline employee. The crime? A delayed flight. A gate change. A missing bag. Basically, the kind of inconvenience that makes you sigh, not the kind that requires lashing out an employee just trying to do their job.

The expectation seems to be perfection. People want their travel experience to be seamless, frictionless, and catered to their every whim—as if airlines are five-star spas in the sky. The moment something goes wrong they explode. The gate agent, the flight attendant, the poor soul scanning boarding passes suddenly becomes the villain in their personal drama.

Yelling doesn't make the plane fly faster, doesn't teleport your luggage, and doesn't magically summon a pilot from the break room. It just makes everyone around you uncomfortable and, in some cases, gets law enforcement involved.

And it's not just airports. I talk about this in my other *Crazy!* books because the stage is everywhere: checkout lines, customer service counters, cruise ships, restaurants, roadways, even golf courses. Anywhere people interact with other people, there's potential for conflict—and potential for grace.

If you have a problem with an employee, here's an idea: seek out the manager, speak calmly, explain the issue, and ask for help. You might be shocked at how far a little kindness goes. That employee is probably following protocol, doing exactly what they were trained to do.

Kindness is still contagious. Decency still matters. And no one ever looked cool yelling at a gate agent.

## Taking Too Many Snacks

**But they're free!** That's the excuse, right? "It's free, so why not?"

But here's the thing: those snacks are meant for everyone. Not just the guy in 9B who's building a personal snack tower.

Taking one or two? Totally fine. Grabbing four or five, then eating only one and leaving the rest like some kind of trail mix graveyard? That's just greedy—and wasteful.

It's not a buffet. It's a courtesy. If you're that hungry, bring your own snacks. That way you get exactly what you want, and you won't be raiding the communal cookie jar like a raccoon in a pantry.

Besides, your seatmate probably had their eye on that last bag of pretzels before you swooped in like a snack ninja.

You're not going to starve. It's a two-hour flight, not a survival expedition. You'll land. There will be food. You'll live.

Bottom line: One or two snacks. No hoarding. No crinkling symphonies. No snack pyramids. And if you must indulge, do so with dignity.

By the way, nothing is "free."

# Long Lines at Security

**Oh no! You're late. Again.** You sprint from the car to the terminal, dodge a family of five with matching neck pillows, and arrive at check-in—only to find a line that stretches to the next town.

Come on, you knew this was coming. Peak travel time, holiday crowds, and the universal law of "Murphy's Airport" guarantee it. So, next time, give yourself a buffer. A big one.

Sometimes the delay isn't your fault. Not enough clerks. A surprise security drill. Overweight bags. Or a traveler who packed their emotional support bowling ball. It happens.

Occasionally, a kind TSA agent waves those with flights leaving in twelve minutes and sweat stains to prove it. Unfortunately, this system relies on honesty, and some folks treat it like an improv audition: "I swear my gate is closing!"

Plan for the worst, hope for the best, and remember—stress loves a tight schedule. Give it less to work with.

# Talkative Passengers

**And did you hear about...** You've settled in for your flight and all you want to do is read, maybe catch a nap. But no—you have a seatmate who wants to talk. Not converse, mind you. Just talk. Nonstop. To you. At you.

Some people are naturally chatty. Others are nervous flyers, and talking is their way of venting. Either way, it's a one-way street—and you're the toll booth.

Some people feel compelled to talk to anyone who'll listen. But most travelers prefer peace. They might be friendly, or they might be calming their nerves.

If you do strike up a conversation, you'll know quickly if it's welcome. A warm reply that invites more? Great. A polite nod or a one-word answer? Time to zip it. Headphones are the international symbol for "Leave me alone."

If it's an early morning or late-night flight and the cabin's quiet, maybe take the hint—and the nap. Either way, respect their space.

And if someone does try to chat, a polite "I'm going to rest now" usually does the trick. If you do engage, keep the volume low. We're all sharing this tin can in the sky.

It is commonly accepted to respect one's "space." If, however, you do engage in a conversation, try to keep volume low.

I once had a gentleman sitting next to me on a flight begin talking to me, but I wasn't really in the mood. I decided I would be polite and at least talk for a minute or two. It turned out he was from my hometown. The more we talked, the more we enjoyed sharing our childhood experiences. And before we knew it, the plane began its approach to our destination.

You never know...

# Calling for Attendant Too Many Times

**What do you want this time?** A pillow? A second Margarita? A philosophical debate about the armrest?

Flight attendants are trained professionals, not your airborne butlers. They've got hundreds of passengers to care for, safety protocols to follow, and turbulence to dodge. Yet somehow, you need a personal concierge service at 35,000 feet?

Most travelers board, sit quietly, and disembark without incident. But then there's that person—the serial summoner. Maybe they're used to having an assistant. Maybe they think the call button is a remote control for comfort. Either way, it's time for a reality check.

Thou shalt not treat the flight attendant like a genie. Three wishes per flight, max.

Unless your seat is on fire or your neighbor is trying to baptize you with tomato juice, you can probably wait. Sit back, relax, and let the crew handle actual emergencies.

## Inattentive Parents

**They're around somewhere. Why do you ask?** You've seen them—the parents who seem to believe that once they enter an airport, their job is done. Their children become free-range humans, roaming terminals, climbing furniture, and screaming at the top of their lungs.

Meanwhile, the parents are either buried in their phones or blissfully unaware, as if parenting were a coat they checked at security.

Most of us have raised children or survived the toddler years with some measure of dignity. We know it's not easy. But public behavior still matters, and it doesn't happen by accident. It requires something called "parenting"—a hands-on activity that, shockingly, doesn't take time off.

Yes, the kids may be loud, messy, or mildly feral. But the real issue isn't them—it's the adults who've decided that discipline is optional in public spaces. You can't blame a five-year-old for acting like a five-year-old. You can blame the grown-up who's pretending not to notice.

If these pint-sized tornadoes are driving you crazy, do your best to keep your cool. Don't be the airport vigilante who confronts the parents or scolds the kids. That's not going to help anyone—and it'll only turn Gate 32 into a gladiator arena.

## Drunk Passengers

**Hit me again, bartender!** When your flight's delayed and you're stuck in the terminal for hours, it's tempting to pass the time with a drink or two. A little alcohol can calm the nerves and make the wait more bearable. But let's not confuse "a drink" with "a bender." There's a fine line between relaxed and rowdy, and once you cross it, you're not just a nuisance—you're a hazard.

And chances are the person who's been throwing back shots at the gate always ends up sitting next to you. They're already marinated in rum, and the first thing they do after takeoff is order another drink. You brace yourself for the slurred speech, the unsolicited life story, and the looming threat of turbulence-induced upchuck. Even the smell of overindulgence can make nearby passengers nauseous. And if they've really gone off the rails, you start wondering how long before they're yelling at the flight attendant or trying to open the emergency exit mid-flight.

Drunk passengers can be rude, obnoxious, combative, and downright dangerous. It's not just annoying—it's a safety issue. If someone becomes violent or causes damage, criminal charges can follow. Airlines don't mess around: intoxicated passengers can be denied boarding with no refund, removed mid-flight, banned from future travel, and even billed for the cost of a diverted plane. That's one expensive cocktail.

> **Did you know:** Under federal law, airlines have the right to refuse to board passengers who are visibly intoxicated or pose a risk to themselves, the crew, or other passengers. This is outlined in 49 U.S. Code § 46504, which prohibits interference with the duties of flight crew members, including being disruptive or belligerent due to intoxication. (Source: JettonMeredithLaw.com)

Gate agents and flight attendants are trained to spot the signs—slurred speech, unsteady movements, disruptive behavior—and they're empowered to act before things escalate. If you notice someone clearly intoxicated boarding the plane or sitting nearby, speak up. Better to handle it on the ground than deal with chaos in the sky.

So, do us all a favor: wait until you reach your destination to get hammered. And if you're driving afterward, maybe skip the bar altogether. Your liver, fellow passengers, and others on the road will be appreciative.

# Body Odor

**Have you heard of a thing called a "shower?"** I don't care if someone chooses not to bathe. That's their business. But when they decide to share their personal funk with the rest of us on a four-hour flight? That's where I draw the line.

Here's the problem: people with natural body odor often can't smell themselves. To them, they're fine. To the rest of us, they're a human cheese wheel marinating in misery. A fart may stink, but it passes. A loud chewer eventually stops eating. But body odor? It lingers. It clings. It colonizes your nostrils like a hostile invader.

And wouldn't you know it—on your particular flight, the one person who hasn't bathed since COVID ends up sitting next to you. Fantastic!

Offer the offender a stick of deodorant with a smile and a prayer. Spray air freshener like you're fogging for mosquitoes. Fashion a clothespin mask and pretend it's a new TSA mandate.

Better yet, let's add a new rule to flying: "No passenger shall board an aircraft without first passing the sniff test administered by a neutral third party (preferably a Labrador Retriever)."

And for those who sweat under stress—pack a stick of deodorant in your carry-on. It's not just hygiene. It's diplomacy.

## Excessive Cologne

**Did you spill the bottle?** On the flip side of body odor is the passenger who bathes in cologne, marinates in scented lotion, or slathers on hand sanitizer like it's a spa day at 30,000 feet.

Sometimes the smell is so overpowering you can't breathe. And when you finally escape the cabin, you're wearing their fragrance like a badge of trauma.

Which is worse—BO or Eau de Overkill? Tough call. Either way, the solution might be the same. Clothespin, anyone?

Let's not forget that some passengers have allergies, asthma, or sensory sensitivities. A whiff of your "Ocean Thunder" body spray might trigger migraines, coughing fits, or a full-blown revolt in Row 17.

So, here's a simple rule: Do not wear or apply strong scents on an airplane. I repeat...DON'T! You're not impressing anyone and it's offensive.

## Reclining Seats

**Whoa, wait, what are you doing?** On long flights, reclining can be a blessing, offering a more comfortable position for rest or sleep. But for the person behind you, it might feel more like a curse.

There you are, enjoying your carefully balanced tray of airplane cuisine when suddenly, the seat in front of you lunges backward. Your drink spills, your food flies, and your mood nosedives. Thanks a lot!

Yes, reclining is allowed. If the seat reclines, it's fair game. In Economy, the movement is minimal anyway. But just because you can recline doesn't mean you should do so without a little courtesy.

Before you lean back, take a moment to check on the person behind you. Are they eating? Do they have a full tray? Are they tall, broad-shouldered, or mobility-challenged?

During meal service, keep your seat upright. On short flights, skip the recline altogether. On long-haul journeys, reclining is expected—but still, do it slowly. A sudden jolt can send drinks flying and tempers flaring. And if someone reclines into your space, don't retaliate with seat-punching or passive-aggressive nudges.

That's not etiquette—it's air rage.

# Airplane Food

**Aaaah…I've been looking forward to this meal!** For years, airplane meals were the highlight of the flight—tiny trays of mystery meat and surprise sides that somehow made cruising at 35,000 feet feel like a dinner party. But thanks to regulations, health concerns, and relentless cost-cutting, Economy-class cuisine has devolved into something resembling hospital food. And in some cases, worse.

Now, I'm not talking about first or business class, where—depending on the airline—you might be served a well-crafted meal with actual flavor. I'm talking about Economy. The rest of us. Where the "meal" (if it's served at all) looks like a miniature replica of real food, as if someone shrunk a TV dinner and removed the seasoning for safety.

Airplanes may be marvels of engineering and among the safest environments in terms of air flow. Air circulates downward and is regularly refreshed, and most passengers have their

32

personal vents blasting like mini wind tunnels. But dining in this environment? Not ideal.

Add to that the lower cabin pressure and desert-dry air, which inflame your glands and dull your senses. You're left with about 70% of your normal taste perception. That's right—your gourmet chicken tikka masala now tastes like warm cardboard with a hint of cumin.

But at least it's something to do!

## Arm Rests

**I called dibs!** Ever been stuck in the middle seat on a flight, only to discover that both armrests have mysteriously vanished into the elbows of your neighbors? It's one of those silent battles that plays out thousands of feet in the air.

So, what's the rule here, you ask? In a typical three-seat row, there are four armrests. The window and aisle seats each have one outer armrest, leaving the two inner ones up for grabs. Some believe the middle seat deserves both. Others believe possession is nine-tenths of the law.

In my opinion the middle seat gets both inner armrests because the aisle seat has easy access and legroom, and the window seat gets a view and a wall to lean on. The middle seat, widely considered the least desirable, deserves a little compensation. But not everyone agrees, and that's where things get awkward. One trick to avoid the armrest tug-of-war is to lift the armrest entirely, reclaiming a sliver of space and avoiding conflict.

Still, armrest ownership remains one of travel's great unsolved mysteries. So, I suggest a little diplomacy: talk to your seatmates, establish boundaries, and maybe even negotiate a treaty before takeoff.

## Leaving Trash in Seat-Back Pockets

**I'll just stuff it in here!** That seems to be the lazy mantra of too many airline passengers who treat the seat-back pocket like their personal trash bin. But let's be clear—leaving garbage behind on a plane is more than just inconsiderate; it's downright disrespectful.

Flight attendants already make several trips up and down the aisle collecting trash before landing. Choosing to ignore those opportunities and instead cramming your refuse into the seat-back pocket only adds to their workload. Why? Because it's convenient for you? That's not convenience—it's carelessness.

There's absolutely no reason to do this. You can always take your trash with you and drop it in a receptacle as you exit the plane. It's not hard.

What's worse, this behavior isn't just rude—it's unhygienic. Those pockets are used by the next passenger to store their phone, book, or snack.

Leaving behind tissues, wrappers, or worse, chewed gum, turns a shared space into a biohazard. And yes, someone actually thought it was okay to stick their gum in the emergency pamphlet. Seriously?

It's time to take responsibility for your belongings—and that includes your trash. Flying is a shared experience. Let's not make it worse for the next person or the hardworking crew who keeps things running smoothly. Do the right thing. Clean up after yourself. The sky's the limit, but your garbage shouldn't be.

# Watching Movies
# Without Headphones

**Turn it down, please!** Watching a movie without headphones on an airplane? Really? Come on—people are trying to sleep, read, or simply enjoy a quiet flight without being subjected to your action flick's explosions or non-stop banter.

Most airlines provide headphones or encourage you to use your own, and the seatback screens are designed to work with them. It's not just polite—it's basic courtesy.

It's baffling, really. You're surrounded by crying babies, snoring seatmates, and the crunch of pretzels—and you still think the solution is to add your movie's soundtrack to the mix? No. The solution is earbuds. Plug in, tune out, and enjoy your film like a civilized traveler. Otherwise, you're broadcasting your lack of awareness to the entire cabin.

So, grab the headphones, press play, and keep your audio to yourself. Because if you don't, well…let's not go there.

## Standing Up During Turbulence

**Whoa, this is challenging!** Turbulence hits and suddenly someone's up and wandering the cabin like it's a stroll through the park. Are they thrill-seeking? Confused?

Standing during turbulence isn't brave—it's stupid. You're not just risking your own limbs, you're a human bowling ball waiting to strike an unsuspecting aisle-sitter. Flight attendants, trained professionals that they are, often stay seated during rough patches. If they're buckled in, you should be too.

And if you're up when the bumps begin? Hustle back to your seat like it's musical chairs and the music just stopped. Buckle up. Stay put.

Need to use the bathroom? Unless it's a code-red emergency, maybe wait. Navigating a restroom during turbulence is like trying to thread a needle on a rollercoaster. Not exactly a graceful experience.

Also, beware the overhead bins—turbulence can pop them open like surprise party favors. Only instead of confetti, you get a laptop to the face.

Stay seated, stay safe, and save your daredevil antics for land-based adventures. The sky's wild enough without you adding to the chaos.

## Cramped Seat Space

**Cozy, huh?** What's with the ever-shrinking seats and vanishing leg room? Airlines seem determined to squeeze every last inch—and every last passenger—into these flying sardine cans.

Smaller planes? Tighter seating. By cramming in more seats, airlines boost profits, reduce emissions (fewer flights, more bodies), and maybe lower fares if you don't mind sitting like a folded napkin.

Sure, the seat dimensions may only be an inch or two smaller, but the leg room? That's where the real squeeze happens. In many cases, the space between rows has shrunk by up to six inches. Even the seat width has taken a hit. All in the name of profit.

Meanwhile, the average passenger has grown taller, wider, and less thrilled about playing human origami.

**Did you know:** "Every other place where you look at the seating, the seats have gotten bigger to match the fact that people are getting bigger," Hudson said. "If you look at theaters, you look at automobile seats, [or] any other venue seats have gotten larger. Only on airlines have they gotten smaller. So, they're going the opposite way from where the human body is going." (Source: Mack, DeGeurin, Popular Science, Popsci.com)

And let's talk safety. In an emergency, tight seating means slower exits and more chaos, not to mention the germ-sharing bonanza that comes with shoulder-to-shoulder seating.

For larger people, these seats aren't just uncomfortable—they're borderline impossible.

If it's a short flight and the fare's a steal, maybe the discomfort is worth it. Me? I'll take the extra space any day. Call me old-fashioned, but I like breathing room with my peanuts.

Profit over comfort, folks!

## Airplane Noise

**Wait? Can you name that sound?** Air travel is noisy. Not just "background hum" noisy—more like "industrial symphony" noisy.

From the moment you board, the plane begins its mechanical overture: fans whirring, vents hissing, and that ever-present hum of the auxiliary power unit (APU), keeping the cabin cool and the lights on while you wait to taxi.

The engines spool up, the flaps adjust with a groan, and the plane begins its slow roll toward the runway. You'll hear clunks, whirs, and the occasional mystery thud—each one perfectly normal.

Takeoff is the main event. The engines roar to full power, the cabin vibrates, and for a few seconds, it feels like you're strapped to a rocket. Once airborne, the sound settles into a steady drone—less dramatic, but still loud enough to make conversation a lip-reading exercise.

Mid-flight, if the plane changes altitude, the engines may surge again. You might hear the flaps adjust or the landing gear shift. These sounds are routine, but if you're not expecting them, they can be concerning.

Landing brings gear deployment, flap movement, engine modulation, and finally, the satisfying bump of tires hitting tarmac. Reverse thrusters kick in with a whoosh, slowing the plane to a crawl. You've arrived—ears ringing, nerves intact.

> **Did you know:** There are four key sources of noise and sensations from takeoff. These include the engines, flaps, landing gear, and aerodynamic noise. The engines create strong acceleration, like pushing the pedal to the floor in an automobile. This is completely necessary, as the engines need to propel a lumbering aircraft that may weigh over a million pounds to speeds of approximately 170 miles/hour (274 Km/hour) in a short distance. The noises that are heard from the engines are the result of the shearing of air masses. Simply, the high-speed air coming out of the engines is smashing into stationary air outside and it causes noise. (Source BackPacker.org)

For some, these sounds are stressful. For others, they're just part of the ride. Earplugs help. So, do noise-canceling headphones. But sometimes, the best strategy is simply understanding what you're hearing. Ask an attendant if you'r concerned. Once you know the cues, the noises become less alarming—and maybe even a little reassuring.

And then, after all the roaring and rumbling, comes the most welcome sound of all: The sound of silence.

## Air Pressure

**My head is going to explode!** Cabin pressure on an airplane is one of those sneaky little things that affects some passengers more than others. One minute you're sipping ginger ale, the next your ears feel like they're going to burst.

You try everything—chewing gum like a cow, sucking on candy like it's a life-saving lozenge, yawning and swallowing so often you start to wonder if you're part pelican. And still...pop, already!

But it's not just your ears. That thin, recycled air can leave you feeling like you've just run a marathon in a sauna—mild fatigue, fuzzy thinking, and the sudden urge to nap like a toddler after a juice box.

And if you've got high blood pressure? Don't wing it. Talk to your doctor before you fly, and keep your meds handy. The only thing worse than a delayed flight is a delayed prescription.

**Did you know:** Cabin pressurization is important because of the nuances between low- and high-altitude air density. Air is less dense at high altitudes than low altitudes. At ground level, the air pressure is a little over fourteen pounds per square inch (PSI). When an airplane reaches its typical cruising altitude—usually about 30,000 to 40,000 feet—the air pressure may be just 4 to 5 PSI.

The low air pressure associated with high-altitude flights can restrict passengers from receiving an adequate amount of oxygen unless the cabin is pressurized. Low air pressure means the air is less dense. Therefore, it contains less oxygen. If airplanes didn't pressurize their cabins, it could lead to insufficient oxygen as well as related medical problems like hypoxia. Airplanes need pressurized cabins because it ensures passengers, as well as crew members, receive an adequate amount of oxygen in the air they breathe. (Source: monroeaerospace.com)

So, next time you board, remember: it's not just the crying baby or the guy next to you who thinks deodorant is optional that may be causing issues—it may the cabin pressure, too.

# Dehydration

**Cotton mouth here!** Flying dries you out—fast. Cabin humidity can plummet to 10–20%, turning your mouth into a desert and your sinuses into sandpaper.

That dry air? Your nasal defenses weaken, making you a prime target for airborne bugs.

Feeling parched, foggy, or dizzy? You're probably dehydrated. The fix is simple: drink water. Lots of it. Skip the booze and even the caffeine—they're dehydrators in disguise.

> **Did you know:** Don't wait until feeling thirsty to drink water. By the time a person feels thirsty, they may already be dehydrated. Start hydrating well at least 24 hours in advance of a flight. Drink lots of water during the flight and avoid overconsumption of caffeinated or alcoholic drinks that can make dehydration worse.
> (Source: CenterforFamilyMedicine.com)

Extreme cases? Pack a personal humidifier. Yes, they exist. And while you're at it, move. Walk the aisle. Spell the alphabet with your feet. Long flights can mess with circulation.

Basically, drink water and move your legs.

## Boarding Chaos

**Coming through!** Boarding a plane should be simple. The gate agent calls your group, you get in line, and you board. Simple, right? But somehow, this turns into a full-contact sport.

The moment the first group is called, a crowd surges forward—people who know they're not next but just can't resist the gravitational pull. They clog the entryway, glare at anyone trying to pass, and shuffle just enough to pretend they're not blocking the path.

Recently, I watched a textbook case unfold. The gate agent called for airline credit card holders. A dozen folks lined up. Thirty seconds later, a few more joined. Then more. Within minutes, it was a free-for-all. The logic? "Well, if they're doing it, so can we." And just like that, those of us waiting patiently were punished for following the rules.

Why the rush? Your seat isn't going anywhere. The plane won't leave without you. And if you board last, you avoid the aisle traffic jam and the awkward dance of squeezing past people already settled in. Relax, people—we're all going to the same place.

Airlines have tried everything to tame the chaos: boarding by group, by seat location, by cabin class, by loyalty status. Some board window seats first, then middle, then aisle. Brilliant—no more climbing over strangers. Others board back-to-front, which also makes sense. But no matter the method, there's always a crowd of gate lurkers hovering like it's general admission at a rock concert.

Some airlines now scan boarding passes to verify your group before you're allowed through. If you jump the gun, you'll be flagged and held back while your actual group boards. Technology to the rescue—finally!

Still, the bin space battle rages on. People jockeying for overhead bin supremacy. If you want early access, you can pay for it. If you don't want to pay, don't push. Simple.

And then there's the "miracle mobility" phenomenon. You see someone strolling through the food court, browsing tech gadgets, and then—poof!—they're in a wheelchair for preboarding. I'm not saying everyone's faking it, but let's just say some folks are playing the system while others with genuine needs get sidelined. That's not just frustrating—it's disrespectful.

So, stay seated until your group is called. Don't be a gate lurker. Don't be a bin hog. Don't be a miracle walker. Just chill.

We're all going to the same place. Let's try arriving with our dignity intact.

## Lack of Sleep

**I'm trying to sleep here!** Most people just want to snooze through the flight, wake up at their destination, and pretend the whole ordeal never happened.

But sleeping on a plane? Easier said than done. Between the engine hum, turbulence, aisle traffic, crying babies, loud talkers, aggressive chewers, mysterious odors, and the captain's announcements that always interrupt your sleep—rest is elusive.

It's wonderful the person next to you is enjoying a deep, restorative slumber. Less so when their snoring sounds like a chainsaw in a wind tunnel.

Still, sleep can be achieved with a little strategy. The window seat is prime real estate: you can lean against the wall, control the shade, and avoid being climbed over. Of course, you risk becoming someone's human pillow, pinned against the fuselage like a pressed flower.

Dress comfortably. Use a neck pillow. Listen to white noise or soothing music. Recline your seat slightly (unless you're in front of me—then don't even think about it!). A mild over-the-counter sleep aid might help, assuming you don't wake up mid-flight thinking you're still at home.

And don't forget the time zone trap. You might land feeling refreshed and ready to go—only to discover it's 3 a.m. and everyone else is asleep. Congratulations, you're now the wide-eyed zombie wandering the streets of Tampa.

Sleep well, if you can.

## Compulsive Leg-Shaking

**A one, and a two...** I get it—flying can be nerve-wracking. The engines roar, the cabin rattles, and your seatmate is clutching their armrest like it's the last lifeboat on the Titanic.

But there's always that one person—always—who decides to tap-dance their way through turbulence with a nonstop leg shake. And somehow, that person is magnetically drawn to sit next to, or directly behind, me.

Now, let's be fair. If it's a medical condition like Restless Leg Syndrome (RLS), I offer nothing but compassion. But if it's just nerves, anxiety, or a misguided attempt to generate in-flight electricity, we need to talk.

I'm perfectly fine with a little leg-jitter during takeoff and landing. Those are high-drama moments. But if your leg is still doing the Macarena over Illinois, we may have a problem.

If you're a shaker, try channeling that energy into something less seismic. Deep breaths. Meditation. Count the number of times the flight attendant says "chips or pretzels" Or better yet, pretend you're a statue. Statues don't shake.

If you're the innocent bystander whose seat is now a vibrating massage chair—don't despair. Redirect your focus. Watch a movie. Listen to music. Imagine you're on a gentle rollercoaster.

Or, if you're lucky, fall asleep and dream of a world where knees stay still and seats remain upright.

## Annoyed Over Bathroom Visits

**Didn't you just go?** There's nothing quite like being trapped in the aisle seat next to someone with a bladder that operates on a five-minute timer.

You've finally settled in—headphones on, tray table down, snack opened—and here comes the dreaded tap on the shoulder: "Sorry, I need to use the restroom." Again. You sigh, do the awkward seat shuffle, gather your belongings like a refugee fleeing a war zone, and perform the aisle yoga routine. Then, just as you've reassembled your life and reclined two degrees, they're back. Round two.

Now, before you start plotting revenge with a strategically spilled ginger ale, take a breath. Maybe they've got a medical issue. Maybe they're nervous. Maybe they just really, really like the bathroom. Whatever the reason, odds are they're not thrilled about this either. Nobody dreams of spending half a flight doing the conga line to the restroom.

If you're a frequent flyer with a weak bladder, do us all a favor and book the aisle seat. That's your express lane to relief without the guilt trip. Sure, you might get clipped by the beverage cart or used as a leaning post by every passenger heading to the back, but that's the price of freedom. Better a bruised elbow than the wrath of a window-seated stranger with a crossword puzzle and a grudge.

And if you're the one being climbed over, try to channel your inner Zen master. The flight will end. Your knees will recover. And one day, it might be you doing the aisle cha-cha with a sheepish smile and a full bladder.

In the meantime, let's all agree on one thing: if you're in the window seat and you know you're going to need to go more than once, maybe skip the scenic view and opt for the aisle. Or at least bring snacks for your row mates. Bribery goes a long way at 35,000 feet.

# Overhead Bin Abuse

**This looks like a good spot!** Overhead bin abuse is one of my top peeves (and I'm guessing yours as well!) when boarding a plane. It's maddening when you're the one hunting for space, but I'll admit, it can be oddly entertaining if you're just watching the chaos unfold.

With airlines charging for checked bags, more passengers are trying to avoid fees by cramming everything into carry-ons. This has turned the overhead bins into prime real estate—and the competition is fierce. Some folks, seated in the back of the plane, will selfishly place their bags in the front bins so they can grab them quickly and bolt when the plane lands. Convenient for them, sure. But it leaves the passengers actually seated in those rows scrambling for space.

My daughter once had to stow her bag ten rows behind her seat because the bin above her was already full. When it came time to deplane, she politely asked the woman in the middle seat to let her out so she could retrieve her bag. Instead, the woman stayed put and let the entire rear cabin pass by. Apparently, common courtesy had deplaned early.

Let's review some basic bin etiquette. First, place your bag in the bin above your own seat.

Radical concept, I know. Second, the overhead bin is not your personal closet—it's *one* carry-on per passenger. Oversized bags and multiple items hog space and leave others stranded. Blankets and coats? They don't belong in the bin. Put them on your lap, on top of your bag, or ask a flight attendant for help. And if you see someone struggling to lift their bag into the bin, don't just sit there with your earbuds in—lend a hand.

Oh, and one more thing: don't rearrange other people's bags without asking. This isn't a game of overhead bin Tetris. Flight attendants do their best to manage the madness, but they can't be everywhere at once.

So, please, be considerate. Use the space above your seat, help your fellow travelers, and remember—the overhead bin is shared space. Let's not turn it into a battleground.

## Cell Phones

**Hello?** I often end up next to someone who just can't stay off their phone. I'm not talking about playing games or texting—I mean full-blown conversations. They're yakking away until the wheels leave the ground, and the moment we descend below 10,000 feet, they're back at it, chatting like they're on a talk show.

Sure, maybe it helps pass the time. But from what I've observed, these are folks who can't stop talking. A quick call? Fine. But an hour-long monologue? That's not a conversation—it's a hostage situation.

> **Did you know:** The reality is that phones haven't interfered with in-flight electrical systems or terrestrial wireless services for decades. The actual reason you're turning on airplane mode is for your fellow passengers. (Source: qz.com)

When the cabin door closes, we're all instructed to switch our phones to "airplane mode." Why? Because cell phones can interfere with the aircraft's communication and navigation systems. Yes, technology has improved, and planes are more resilient now—but the rule still stands. It's not just a suggestion; it's a legal requirement in the U.S.

So, do us all a favor. Flip the switch. Take a break from the phone—and give the rest of us a break from your one-sided TED Talk.

We're all trapped in this aluminum tube together. Let's make it a little more bearable, shall we?

# Loud talking

**Yes, we can ALL hear you!** There's always one. The airborne broadcaster. The high-altitude town crier. The person who thinks the airplane cabin is their personal podcast studio—except none of us subscribed. Whether it's a restaurant, a bar, or a Boeing 737, some people are just naturally loud. Maybe they don't know it. Maybe they're hard of hearing. Or maybe they just believe the world is their audience and we're all lucky to be in the front row. Uh, we're not.

Unlike a bar or restaurant, you can't just move to another table. You're strapped in with nowhere to go and a voice bouncing off every surface like it's auditioning for surround sound. The cabin acoustics? Perfect for amplifying nonsense. Headphones help. Earbuds are a blessing. But if you forgot them, you're stuck learning about their sister's gallbladder surgery, their brother's fantasy football team, or why someone's cousin's neighbor's dog is afraid of cucumbers.

If the loudmouth happens to be telling a delightful story—rare, but not impossible—you might forgive the volume. But let's be honest: most of the time, it's not Shakespeare. It's just loud. So, what can you do? Don't engage. Attention is fuel.

Deny them the oxygen. If you're feeling brave, offer a polite suggestion: "Hey, would you mind lowering your voice a bit?" Translation: "Please stop shouting about your colonoscopy." And if all else fails, summon the flight attendant. That's what they're there for.

And don't forget to check your own volume. If your seatmate can hear you, great. If the pilot can hear you, tone it down. It's a shared tube in the sky. So, if you want to chat it up, keep it down.

## Poaching the Empty Middle Seat

**I think I'll claim this one!** Ah, the middle seat. That lonely, unloved patch of upholstery wedged between two strangers, where elbow room is a myth and personal space is a distant dream.

Most of us avoid it like a middle school cafeteria seat next to the kid with the tuna sandwich. But sometimes, just sometimes, the middle seat is empty—and that's when temptation strikes.

Enter the seat poacher: the bold traveler who eyes that vacant spot like a hawk circling a field mouse. Poaching, in airline terms, is the act of slipping into an unassigned seat—usually a window or aisle—in hopes of scoring a better view, more legroom, or a chance to sit next to your travel companion without coughing up the extra fee. It's a time-honored tradition, a delicate dance of timing, stealth, and plausible deniability.

But before you make your move, remember: the cabin crew are trained in the ancient art of seat assignment enforcement. That empty seat may look like a gift from the travel gods, but it's not yours until a flight attendant gives the nod. Always ask first. And even then, know your boundaries—poaching is only permitted within your assigned section. Crossing into Economy Plus from Economy Basic is a high-risk maneuver, often resulting in a polite but firm exile back to your original seat.

If you're poaching to sit with family, you might earn some sympathy. If you're just dodging the dreaded middle, be prepared for karmic turbulence. And if someone actually chooses the middle seat, offer them your snack mix in tribute—they are either a saint, a masochist, or late to check-in.

If you have an emoty middle seat next to you, ask your seatmate to share the space.

So, poach if you must, but poach with grace. And remember: the skies may be friendly, but the seating chart is sacred.

# Playing Games with Sound On

**Bam! Pow! Zap! Zing!** Playing games on your phone or tablet is a wonderful way to pass the time when flying. But here's the thing—we don't all need to hear the action. Airplanes are already filled with enough noise: the roar of the engines, conversations, crying babies, snack crunching, and the occasional rhythmic foot tap. In this airborne symphony of sound, silence isn't just appreciated—it's desired.

Throughout this book, I've talked about sound in all its forms. Whether it's mechanical, human, or snack-related, the polite traveler aims to minimize their contribution to the noise. That's why most airlines require passengers to use headphones or earbuds when watching videos or playing games. Still, there are always those who live in their own bubble, blissfully unaware of the audio chaos they're unleashing on their fellow passengers.

If you don't have earbuds, the solution is simple: turn the sound off. Your game might be thrilling, but the rest of us don't need to hear every zing and zap. In a space where silence is golden, being one less source of noise is the kindest thing you can do.

# People Trying to Disembark First

**Get out of my way!** I (don't) love watching the aisle Olympics begin the moment the seatbelt sign goes "ding."

It's like the starting gun at the Olympics. The plane hasn't even reached the gate, and already it's a full-contact sport: elbows flying, backpacks swinging, and passengers lunging for overhead bins like it's Black Friday.

For those of us in aisle seats—congratulations, we've become human speed bumps. We sit there, stoic and bruised, as the eager elite trample past in their quest to be first...to stand. For fifteen minutes. While the plane taxis. Slowly.

Why the rush? Stretching your legs? Sure. But you had hours to do that—unless you were in the middle seat, in which case, condolences. Still, standing prematurely doesn't make the plane unload faster.

Wait your turn. Let the rows ahead of you exit first. It's not just polite—it's efficient. The plane empties like a well-oiled zipper when people follow the unwritten rule of "front first, then back."

Exceptions? Of course. If you've got a tight connection, say so. Most folks will gladly let you pass—especially if you ask nicely and don't treat the aisle like your personal racetrack.

So, next time you fly, resist the urge to leap into the aisle like it's a conga line to freedom. Sit tight. Breathe. And remember: we're all getting off this flying sardine can together.

Disembark with dignity. Your knees—and your fellow passengers—will thank you.

## The Toilet

**Hey! I'm working in here!** Yes, we all enjoy a little solitude now and then, but the airplane restroom isn't your personal retreat. Do your business and get out. Some people vanish into that tiny chamber like they're attending a spa day. Are they constipated? Scrolling? Meditating? Writing a novel? Who knows. But while they're in there, the rest of us are doing the pee-pee dance in the aisle.

The number of bathrooms on a plane is limited. If you're applying makeup, reading a book, or just "hanging out," please do that in your seat. The restroom is not a lounge. When you enter, lock the door. When you leave, make sure it's clean and tidy. And yes—wash your hands. That's still a thing.

If you're waiting to use the bathroom, don't knock. The "occupied" sign is not a suggestion.

Don't yell, either. You're not summoning a ghost. If someone's been in there since takeoff, notify a flight attendant. They're trained to handle everything from turbulence to toilet hogs.

Speaking of which—please wear shoes. The floor is probably wet, and you don't want that mystery moisture soaking into your socks or sloshing around inside your shoes later. Trust me.

Now, about smoking and vaping: don't. Since 2000, lighting up in the plane's restroom has been banned. Vaping joined the no-fly list in 2015. Violators face fines, and possibly arrest. And if you think you're being sneaky, just know that smoke detectors in airplane bathrooms are not decorative.

Turbulence in the lavatory? That's a whole new level of challenge. For guys, it's a test of aim. For gals, it's a rodeo. Either way—brace yourself and hope for the best.

Of course, there are exceptions to all of this. Some passengers may need extra time due to medical issues, mobility challenges, changing a diaper, or bandages. Others might be using the space to manage stress or anxiety. And yes, there's always the "Mile High Club." If two people go in and giggle on the way out, we all know.

Be swift. Be clean, close the seat lid, and don't forget to flush.

# Kicking and Bumping the Seat Back

**Do you get a kick out of flying?** Some passengers clearly do—especially the ones who treat the back of your seat like a bongo drum. This ranks high on the list of airborne annoyances, right up there with hogging the armrest and clipping toenails (yes, people do that!).

It's often young children who are the culprits—blissfully unaware that their rhythmic thumping is driving the person in front of them crazy! In those cases, we can only hope for a swift parental intervention.

I recently witnessed a grandmother spring into action when her grandson began a backseat assault. She needed all of one second to shut it down and explain why it wasn't okay. Bravo, Grandma. You're cleared for takeoff.

Now, an occasional bump while retrieving a bag from under the seat? Okay. But repeated jabs? That's turbulence of a different kind.

If you find yourself on the receiving end of a footsie frenzy, start with a polite word to the person behind you. If that doesn't work, summon a flight attendant. If all else fails, close your eyes, breathe deeply, and pretend you're getting a complimentary in-flight massage. (No tip required.)

# Switching Seats

**It's time to play musical chairs!** So, you bought a ticket with an assigned seat. You boarded early, stowed your bag, settled in, and maybe even claimed the armrest. Then it begins.

"Excuse me... would you mind switching seats with me?"

Ah yes, the in-flight game show has begun!

If you wanted my seat so badly, why didn't you book it? Maybe I like this seat. Maybe I paid extra for it. Maybe I strategically selected it to avoid the dreaded middle seat and the dreaded middle-seat talker.

Some folks buy the cheapest seat in the back, then work the cabin like a door-to-door salesperson. Others may want to sit next to a friend.

No one is obligated to switch seats. Not for love, not for legroom, not even for a sob story about a tight connection. And if someone says "no," that's not a cue for huffing, puffing, or passive-aggressive sighing. It's a complete sentence.

Now, if you're the one asking to switch, consider the trade. Aisle for aisle? Window for window? That's fair game. But don't offer me a middle seat in the back row next to the bathroom and expect a standing ovation.

Start with a smile. Explain your situation. Ask politely. And if the answer is no, thank them anyway and return to your assigned seat with dignity intact.

Yes, there are valid reasons to request a swap—families separated, medical needs, or a desperate dash to make a connection. But even then, it's a request, not a right.

Sit in the seat you purchased. Don't put others on the spot. We're all going to the same place. Buckle up, breathe deep, and let's skip the drama.

And remember: it's not your seat until you're in it—and even then, it's not up for grabs.

## Clipping Your Nails

**I mean...really?** Of all the places to groom yourself, a cramped, shared airplane cabin is not it. It's hard to imagine any justification for such inconsiderate behavior. What's next—flossing in the aisle?

Yes, believe it or not, some people actually do this. I know—it's baffling.

Now, while there's no official rule against it, a polite and direct approach works best: "Would you mind waiting until we land to finish that?"

Simple, respectful, and hopefully effective.

And, by the way, where do the clipped nails go?

# Removing Shoes

**Pee-yew!** Come on now. Really? You're not at home. You're not at the beach. You're sealed in a metal tube with 200 strangers and recycled air. You can keep your shoes and socks on for two hours—can't you?

As with smoking and farts, we're often blissfully unaware of our own aromatic contributions. But trust me, everyone around you is painfully aware. That "ahhh" moment for your feet is an "ewww" moment for your neighbors.

Sure, some folks claim that removing their shoes improves circulation and helps them relax. That's nice—for them. But if your comfort comes at the cost of someone else's well-being, maybe it's time to rethink your in-flight rituals.

And let's not forget the practical side: most airlines discourage bare feet for reasons that go beyond common decency. Hygiene, for one. Safety, for another. Walking around in socks or barefoot during turbulence, takeoff, or an emergency evacuation? That's not brave—it's barefoot bravado.

If you're seated in an emergency exit row, shoes on is more than etiquette—it's protocol. You're not just a passenger; you're a potential first responder.

In many cultures, bare feet in public are considered disrespectful. So, while you may be airing out your toes, you might also be stepping on someone's sense of decorum.

What's good for you may not be good for others. Keep those shoes on. Thank ewww!

## Paying Attention at Boarding

**Could you repeat that?** Doesn't it seem natural to listen for your boarding group to be called? Apparently, for some travelers, it's not. They're too busy scrolling, snacking, or perfecting their neck pillow placement to notice the announcements echoing through the terminal. It's as if they're waiting for a personal invitation—perhaps a handwritten note delivered by a flight attendant on a silver tray.

These are the folks who've outsourced awareness. They've been so conditioned to being told what to do—"Now boarding Group 5," "Please remove your shoes," "Sir, that's not a carry-on, that's a steamer trunk"—that they've stopped paying attention altogether.

Then comes the moment of panic. Suddenly, they look up, eyes wide, and realize the line is halfway down the jet bridge. That's when they spring into action—not by checking the monitors or listening to the announcements, but by charging the gate like it's a Black Friday sale. "Excuse me! Has Group 4 boarded yet?" they demand, elbowing past those who did pay attention. The gate agent gives a tight smile and says, "Yes, we're on Group 7 now."

Boarding is already a barely controlled stampede. Being ready when it's your turn isn't just courteous—it's a public service.

# Stuffing Bag in Overhead Compartment

**I know it will fit!** You've seen them. You've been behind them. The determined traveler who insists, "It'll fit!"—as they wedge, shove, rotate, and karate-chop their oversized bag into the overhead bin.

Never mind the posted size limits. Never mind the sullen flight attendant silently judging from row 12. Never mind the laws of physics. This bag will fit—even if it means turning it sideways, upside down, or diagonally across two bins like a luggage hammock.

Why do they do it? Because checking a bag is a sign of weakness. Because $35 is highway robbery. Because they once saw a guy fit a cello in the overhead and now believe anything is possible. There's so much available information about carry-on size limits—websites, signs, even those little metal bag testers at the gate—but for some, those are merely suggestions.

These restrictions exist for a reason. Weight balance, safety, and the small matter of not crushing someone's laptop or lapdog. But hey, who needs rules when you've got determination and a duffel bag the size of Delaware?

If your bag requires a team of sherpas, a pulley system, or divine intervention to lift, it's not a carry-on. It's a cry for help.

And for those who block the aisle for seven minutes while performing aerial yoga with their Samsonite, good luck!

## Holding Up Boarding While Talking with the Attendants

**What did you do this weekend?** There's a time and place for catching up with old friends. The jet bridge at 6:45 a.m. with 137 people behind you is not one of them.

I always greet the flight attendant when I board a plane. A warm smile, a cheerful "Good morning!"—it's the least we can do for the people who are about to spend the next three hours with us and our carry-ons.

But then there's that person. You know the one. They reach the aircraft door and suddenly morph into a long-lost pen pal. "So, how was your weekend?" they ask the flight attendant, as if they're at a backyard barbecue and not the bottleneck of a boarding process. "Oh, you went to Napa? I love Napa! Did you try the Merlot at—"

Meanwhile, the rest of us are standing in the aisle like dominoes, backpacks digging into our spines, wondering if we'll ever see the overhead bin space again.

And it doesn't end there. Upon landing, when the seatbelt sign dings and we all rise like caffeinated meerkats, there they are again—parked in the aisle, reminiscing with the crew about their favorite in-flight snack. "Do you still serve those biscotti? I remember when they used to be lemon-flavored!"

Look, we're all for kindness. A smile, a nod, a "thank you for keeping us alive—that's golden. But let's save the heart-to-hearts for after we've cleared the fuselage, shall we?

# Bringing a Small Pet on Board

**Aaawww . . . isn't it cute?** That tiny dog in a tote bag, peeking out with those big eyes, melting hearts. I love that people can bring their small dogs on the plane—it's comforting for the owner, and way more civilized than stuffing poor "Bosun" in the cargo hold like a suitcase.

But if your dog is a nonstop yapper with the lung capacity of a leaf blower, the only thing it's comforting is its own ego. And if you're going to spend the entire flight whispering sweet nothings, adjusting its blankie, and offering it emotional support bacon, you might want to charter a private jet—or at least a soundproof crate.

Now, if your dog is calm, quiet, and better behaved than most toddlers in Economy, by all means, bring it aboard. Just check the airline's rules first. Most require your pup to be in a carrier that fits under the seat in front of you. That carrier counts as your one carry-on, so choose wisely. Oh, and not all animals are welcome in the cabin. So, unless your pet is a certified service animal don't expect a warm welcome.

If your pet flies better than your Uncle Larry after two Bloody Marys, welcome aboard. If not, maybe let them stay home and binge Animal Planet.

# Please Don't Be That Person

**Noooo!** You know the drill. You're at the gate, casually people-watching as the boarding process begins. It's human nature—we all do it. You scan the crowd, mentally sorting fellow passengers into two categories: "Please sit next to me" and "Please, for the love of peanuts, keep walking."

Then you board. You find your seat. You settle in. And as the aisle parade begins, you spot them—the one person you really don't want to sit next to. Maybe it's the oversized backpack. Maybe it's the Bluetooth speaker blaring something that sounds disguised as music. Maybe it's just a vibe. Whatever it is, you start whispering to the travel gods: Not them. Anyone but them.

But of course, fate has a sense of humor. They stop. They smile. They point to the seat next to you. "That's me," they say.

You brace yourself for three hours of armrest warfare, loud chewing, and unsolicited life stories. But then...something unexpected happens. They're actually kind of delightful. You chat. You laugh. You bond over your mutual love for the Dodgers. By the time you land, you're swapping email addresses and promising to stay in touch.

Okay, okay—maybe that's wishful thinking. More often than not, you just hope your seatmate doesn't smell like a gym bag, chew like a goat, or snore like a chainsaw.

So, don't judge too quickly. Air travel is a gamble. Sometimes you win the seatmate lottery. Sometimes you get a middle seat between a talker and a toddler with a tambourine.

Either way, buckle up, be kind, and for everyone's sake—please don't be *that* person.

# Sitting in the Emergency Exit Row

**There's more to it than extra legroom!** Sitting in the emergency exit row on an airplane isn't just about extra legroom—though I'll admit, that's a nice perk for someone with long legs like mine. But there's another reason I choose that seat: I want to be in a position to help others in the event of an emergency. That's part of the deal when you sit there. You're not just a passenger—you're a potential first responder.

That's why it bothers me when I see someone in that row who clearly isn't up to the task. If you're so overweight you can barely move, or if you look like lifting a pencil would be a challenge, then you're not there to help—you're there for the legroom. And that's not okay.

Flight attendants take this seriously. It's part of their safety duties. They'll stop at our row before departing the gate and ask each of us if we're willing and able to assist in an emergency. A verbal "yes" is required—not a nod, not a shrug, not a mumbled "uh-huh." It's a job, and you have to accept it out loud.

So, here's my plea: if you know you can't handle the responsibility, please don't sit in the emergency exit row. It's not just about comfort—it's about safety. Yours, mine, and everyone else's.

## Leaving Garbage Behind

**Somebody will clean it up.** The plane is not a trash can. Repeat: *Not* a trash can.

Yes, somebody will clean it up. But that "somebody" isn't your personal butler—it's a hardworking flight attendant who's already juggling drink orders, turbulence, and passengers who think "airplane mode" is a suggestion.

Throughout the flight, they stroll the aisle like mobile waste collectors, cheerfully offering to take your trash. They even do a final sweep before descent, hoping you'll part ways with your empty chip bag or crumpled napkin.

You can leave trash around your house all you want, but on a plane? Be a decent human. Hand it over when asked. Or take it with you and toss it in one of the many airport trash bins. Excess trash left behind can even create delays.

## Inconsiderate Passengers

**Excuse me?** They stomp through terminals like they're auditioning for a role in "Airport Rage" Their carry-ons are oversized, their tempers flaring, and their sense of decency? Nonexistent. You know the type—they bark at gate agents, shove past elderly passengers, and treat flight attendants like personal butlers with wings.

These aren't your garden-variety annoyances like seat-kickers or armrest hogs. No, these are the full-time professionals of unpleasantness. They wake up rude, sip coffee with a scowl, and board the plane ready to unleash their inner tyrant. If the overhead bin is full, it's a personal attack. If the flight is delayed, it's a conspiracy. If the snack is pretzels instead of cookies, it's grounds for a lawsuit.

I've watched them berate staff for things beyond anyone's control—weather, turbulence, gravity. I've seen them roll their eyes at crying babies, sigh loudly when someone needs help, and act like basic human kindness is a TSA-prohibited item.

And here's the kicker: they're not just having a difficult day. This is their personality. Chronic dissatisfaction wrapped in a fleece neck pillow. They don't just do inconsiderate things—they *are* inconsiderate. Period.

## Smelly and Messy Snacks

**Are those Brussels Sprouts? You're kidding me, right?** "Oh yes, I'll have the Brussels sprouts with extra garlic, please!" said no sane flyer ever. And yet, some airlines actually serve this pungent little cabbage grenade. Smell is one of our most powerful senses—it can transport us to childhood kitchens or straight into a gag reflex.

But airline food is just the beginning. Enter the passengers who bring their own olfactory landmines onboard. I've sat next to someone who unpacked a bag of snacks that smelled like a science experiment gone wrong. Tuna sandwiches, hard-boiled eggs, spicy jerky, anything with curry—these are not just snacks, they're airborne assaults. Add in body odor, smelly feet, and cologne applied with a fire hose, and you've got a sensory cocktail no one ordered.

Then there's the mess factor. Doritos, Cheetos, cheddar popcorn—these snacks don't just smell, they leave behind neon-orange fingerprints on armrests, tray tables, and window shades. It's like a crime scene dusted with cheese. If you crave these foods, enjoy them before or after your flight.

But Brussels sprouts? On a plane? That's just turbulence for the nose.

## Clapping on Landing

**We made it alive! Hurrah!** This one's a bit of a high-altitude hot potato. Some passengers erupt into applause the moment the wheels kiss the tarmac. Why? Relief. Joy. A heartfelt "thank you" to the folks up front. It's a spontaneous celebration of survival—like escaping a bear, but with pretzels.

Others, however, find it cringe-worthy. The clapping can feel performative, disruptive, or even condescending. Some pilots have confessed that it feels like passengers doubted their ability to land the plane in the first place. "Oh wow, you didn't crash us—bravo!"

**Did you know:** Clapping when an airplane lands isn't a universal phenomenon. While it's more common in some regions, it's often seen as a cultural quirk in places like the U.S., Russia, and Israel. In the U.S., we clap for many things— movies, concerts, even when food arrives at the table. It might stem from our tendency to express gratitude or excitement in group settings. But in other cultures, clapping on planes can signify something deeper, such as relief, celebration, or homecoming. (Source: https://www.cheapair.com/blog/why-do-travelers-clap-when-the-airplane-lands-and-why-does-it-bug-some-people/)

Let's be honest: a smooth, uneventful flight is the best kind. No drama. No turbulence. No need for a standing ovation. A polite "thank you" to the crew as you disembark? That'll do nicely.

Still, if clapping helps you release your airborne anxiety or express gratitude, go for it. Just maybe skip the encore.

## Turbulence

**Did we just hit something?** Even on a smooth flight, some passengers find the experience nerve-wracking. Add turbulence, and it can feel like the sky itself is conspiring against you.

Most turbulence is completely normal. It can be caused by flying over mountains, passing through clouds, encountering severe weather, or simply from shifting air currents and thermal changes. Think of it like a bumpy road in the sky—or waves rocking a boat. Uncomfortable? Sure. Dangerous? Rarely.

> **Did you know:** Turbulence does not cause a plane to crash although it creates panic among passengers. Planes are engineered to survive all types of turbulence. Violent turbulences may seem scary. However, pilots are specially trained accordingly. The only thing you need to do is to fasten your seat belt and remain calm until the turbulence ends. You might have an uncomfortable experience for a short time but the planes shake during turbulence and it is regarded as normal. (Source: https://www.flypgs.com/en/travel-glossary/turbulence)

Unless the captain makes an announcement, there's no cause for alarm. You're still cruising safely.

Now, don't be surprised if your seatmate suddenly grabs your arm or leg in a moment of panic. It might startle you at first, but hey—you may have just become their in-flight hero. A little human connection goes a long way at 35,000 feet.

And one last tip: hold onto your beverage. Turbulence may not be dangerous, but a spilled Diet Coke can be a tragedy.

Airplanes are designed to handle turbulance. It may be scary, but it's okay.

# Delays and Cancellations

**Now what do I do?!** Well, we could go on for days with this topic. One of the most frustrating aspects of flying is the uncertainty of whether your flight will actually take off on time—or at all. It's the nature of the beast.

But some passengers treat it like a personal betrayal. These are the same folks who yell at servers when their soup is lukewarm or berate retail clerks over expired coupons. When things don't go their way, someone's gotta pay.

Delays and cancellations cause stress not just for passengers, but for the airport staff too. You might have a connecting flight hanging in the balance, and suddenly your itinerary looks like a game of Jenga. The reasons for these disruptions are many: weather, technical issues, crew availability, late arrival of the plane, strikes, late passengers, medical emergencies, security concerns, congestion, fueling, cleaning, loading—you name it. Most of these are out of the airline's control, and not a secret plot to ruin your vacation.

Think about this: with over 45,000 flights and nearly three million passengers flying each day, even a one percent hiccup means 450 flights and 30,000 people affected. That's a lot of missed weddings, lost luggage, and airport naps. While it may be a disruption in your plans, the airlines are constantly juggling these challenges and doing the best they can to keep things moving.

> **Did you know:** You now are "guaranteed to get your money back when an airline doesn't transport you from point A to B as promised, without having to file any paperwork." (Source: CBS MoneyWatch).

So, don't take it out on the employees. They want you to get where you're going. Things happen. Relax. Stay informed. Don't wait to find out after the fact—check in with the desk or ask a flight attendant if you're already onboard. Sometimes you'll get a heads-up and can plan your alternate route. Install the airline app to stay ahead of the game. And yes, some airlines offer compensation for delays and cancellations, though weather-related delays usually don't qualify.

## It Only Takes One

**Wait!** Everyone's boarded. Bags are stowed. You're buckled in, ready to go. And yet… nothing happens.

You glance around. No commotion. No announcements. Just a plane full of passengers collectively wondering: What's the holdup?

Then comes the whisper: We're waiting for one more. Ah yes—the lone straggler. The human delay. The person who decided that "boarding time" was more of a suggestion than a deadline.

And when they finally arrive? No apology. No urgency. Just a casual stroll down the aisle, as if they're entering a spa.

> **Did you know:(** According to the Department of Transportation (DOT), there are tarmac delay rules that US airlines must follow: Carriers are not allowed to hold a domestic flight on the tarmac for more than three hours and an international flight for more than four hours, barring a couple of exceptions (like if the pilot deems it's for a safety reason). When the delay stretches to the two-hour point, the airline must provide passengers with water and a snack, such as a granola bar. Airlines must also ensure passengers have access to working toilets, any necessary medical care, and that the cabin temperature is comfortable. (Source: cntraveler.com)

Airlines try to accommodate latecomers. But that courtesy can come at a cost—especially for those with tight connections. One person's tardiness becomes everyone else's headache.

Seatmates won't say a word, but their body language will scream: You ruined my day.

# Feeling Sick

**Uh oh...** One of the last things anyone wants mid-flight is to feel sick—or be seated next to someone who does. But let's face it: it happens.

Air travel can be disorienting. Nausea strikes more often than we'd like to admit, and even when someone's prepared, it's still unsettling. Especially when the smell starts to waft through the cabin. That's when things can spiral. One person gets sick, and suddenly it's a domino effect of discomfort.

That's why I always come prepared. Sure, the seat-back pocket usually holds a barf bag (or "air sickness bag" if we're being polite), but I bring my own—just in case. It's discreet, reliable, and ready for action.

I also take motion sickness meds when needed, and sometimes something to ease anxiety. Watching what I eat before flying helps too—no greasy burgers or mystery sushi at the terminal.

If you feel that familiar wave of queasiness, don't tough it out. Let a flight attendant know. They've seen it all and are trained to help.

And most importantly: don't feel embarrassed. This is a normal, human thing. You're not alone. You're just airborne.

# Loud Electronics

**I can't hear myself think!** Somewhere between the roar of the engines, the whoosh of the air vents, and the guy in 17A watching a movie on his phone at full volume, my brain has filed a formal noise complaint.

Why do some people act like they're home alone with a Bluetooth speaker and a bottomless mimosa? This is, not your living room, not your man cave, and definitely not your personal IMAX theater.

Yes, I get it. Airplanes are loud. But that doesn't mean your tablet needs to be louder. If your volume is set to "chainsaw duel in a hurricane," it's time to invest in headphones. Or better yet, try the ancient art of subtitles. We all paid for a seat, not a front-row ticket to your audio extravaganza. Some of us are trying to nap, read, or stare blankly at the seatback map wondering how we're still over Nebraska.

So, here's an idea: if your entertainment can be heard three rows away, you're no longer a passenger—you're the in-flight entertainment. Please see the flight attendant for your complimentary peanuts and cease and desist order.

# Grooming

**How do I look?** There's a sacred space for personal grooming. It's called your bathroom. Not seat 23B. I understand that travel can be chaotic—maybe you sprinted through TSA, dodged a rogue roller bag, and barely made it to your gate. But once you're airborne, the cabin is not your personal powder room.

I've sat next to passengers who treat their seat like a full-service salon. Over the course of a flight, I've witnessed flossing (with gusto), brushing teeth (into a napkin?), applying deodorant (thank you, but...), painting fingernails (fumes, anyone?), wearing moisturizer face masks (terrifying at midnight), applying makeup (with full contouring), tweezing nose hairs (I kid you not), clipping nails (aerial shrapnel), shaving (yes, with a razor), and spraying cologne (now we all smell like "Ocean Thunder").

Now, I do understand—maybe you've got a big meeting, a hot date, or just a deep need to feel fresh. But after fifteen minutes of grooming, I promise: you look great. Really. You've achieved peak airplane fabulous. Now let's all sit back, relax, and enjoy the flight—without exfoliating.

Seriously, you look fine and dandy!

# The Window Shade

**It's bright, isn't it?** You're trying to sleep, watch a movie, or simply avoid being blinded by the sun, and yet the window seat passenger insists on keeping their shade up.

You glance around and notice nearly every other shade is down—except yours. It's generally understood that the person in the window seat holds dominion over the shade, but that doesn't mean the rest of us must suffer in silence.

You can politely ask them to lower it, though be prepared for resistance. Some passengers need the shade open to fend off claustrophobia, while others just enjoy gazing out. That's understandable when there's something to see, but when you're cruising above the clouds and the only view is endless sky, well, then...

If diplomacy fails, you can always appeal to a higher power: the flight attendant. Many airlines require shades to be up during takeoff and landing for safety reasons, but in-flight? That's a gray area. Keeping them closed at the gate helps keep ther cabin cooler.

Shade disputes are common, and while there's no official rulebook, perhaps there should be.

For instance, if the sunbeam has weaponized itself into a retinal assault, the shade must come down. If the view consists solely of blinding fluff, the shade should be lowered. And if the shade must remain open to prevent a panic attack, the passenger should offer a heartfelt apology and a peace offering—ideally something chocolate-based.

Ultimately, flight attendants can make the call. Their decisions are final. So, the next time you find yourself in a battle over brightness, remember: courtesy, chocolate, or a small gift may be your best tools. Thank you.

## Unprofessional Staff

**What's your problem?** Every now and then, you run into an airline employee who seems like they were dragged to work by TSA. No smile. No greeting. Just a vibe that says, "I'd rather be anywhere but here."

I've had both ends of the spectrum check my bags. The cheerful ones beam like runway lights, ask about my day, and when I'm wearing my Army hat, they thank me for my service. The grumpy ones? They treat me like I just asked them to personally carry my luggage to Cleveland. No words. No eye contact. Just a hand out for the ID and a boarding pass tossed back to me like a losing lottery ticket.

Recently, I watched a flight attendant stand in the aisle like a wax figure while passengers fumbled with seat numbers and overhead bins. She looked away, as if helping was against her religion. Meanwhile, her colleagues were hustling like it was the final boarding call for decency.

Look, we all have bad days. But when you're in the service business, you've got to fake it better than a reality show romance.

To be fair, airline staff deal with passengers who think "boarding group" is a suggestion and "personal item" includes a cello. But still—if you can't muster a smile, at least don't weaponize a scowl.

If you encounter an airline employee who's less than accommodating, you've got options. Ask for a supervisor. File a complaint with the Department of Transportation. Or just let the airline know. They want feedback. They need it. Because service, like altitude, is something they're supposed to, and want to, maintain.

But always remember: the skies may not be friendly, but you don't have to be silent.

## Twice the Price?

**Wait. What's this for?** You're browsing flights, and there it is: $49 to paradise! You're practically packed. Then you hit "Continue."

Wait—what's this? A fee for choosing a seat. Another for bringing a bag. A "convenience" fee (for whom?). Taxes, surcharges, and a mysterious "carrier-imposed fee" that sounds like a medieval punishment. Final total: $179.

What happened to your $49 flight? It vanished faster than your legroom.

But it's not just airlines. Restaurants now sneak in "kitchen appreciation" fees. Hotels charge "resort fees" for the privilege of using the lobby. And if you've bought a house lately, you know the closing costs are going to add up quickly!

The price you see is just the bait. The real number? That's the switch.

Airlines use dynamic pricing algorithms that adjust fares in real time based on demand, seat availability, and whether the planets are aligned. Prices can double depending on the day you fly.

Want a deal? Fly on a Tuesday at 5 a.m., pack light, and don't even think about selecting a seat.

The skies may be friendly, but the pricing? That's turbulence you can count on.

Pay now. Fly later. Complain forever.

# Bathroom Dilemma

**Hey! I'm next!** Timing is everything. You've been watching the lavatory like a hawk, waiting for that golden moment when there's no line. Someone exits, and you spring into action. But just as you reach the door, a stealthy passenger from a few rows ahead leaps up and slips in before you. Ugh! And then they stay in there forever. What are they doing—redecorating?

Then there's the classic Economy-class rebel who marches up to the first-class bathroom like they've just been upgraded by divine right. Never mind the curtain or the glares from the front cabin—when nature calls, etiquette apparently goes out the window.

If you can, avoid using the bathroom right after takeoff, during the drink and snack service, or in the final descent. It's also a good idea to give your rowmates a heads-up when you need to get up—especially if they've barricaded themselves in with laptops, snacks, and a blanket fortress. This is one of the reasons I always book an aisle seat.

Of course, the best strategy is to go before you board. And if you have a medical condition that requires frequent visits, don't be shy. Let a flight attendant know. They're usually understanding and can help you navigate the situation with minimal drama.

Get in, get out, and let the next poor soul have their moment of relief. Because up here, we're all just trying to make it to our destination with dignity—and dry pants.

## The Frustrating Wait

**Hurry up and wait!** Flying isn't really about getting somewhere—it's about surviving a series of competitive waiting events. Welcome to the Airport Olympics, where every leg of your journey tests your patience, stamina, and ability to pretend you're fine.

First up: the Security Line Sprint. You dash to the checkpoint only to stand behind a guy who packed his belt, boots, and possibly a bowling ball.

Then comes Gate Hovering, where you stake out a seat like it's beachfront property and glare at anyone who dares sit too close.

Boarding Group Bingo follows, a thrilling game where you're Group 7 and they're calling Group 2. Then Group 3. You wait.

Just when you think you're boarding, the gate agent announces a delay due to "aircraft maintenance," or "weather."

Snack time Roulette begins once airborne—will you get pretzels, cookies, or the dreaded "we've run out"? The suspense is delicious.

My dad used to say, "If you have the time, fly." He also said, "Never trust someone who wears flip-flops to the airport." Both still hold true.

Ironically, the flight itself is often the shortest part of the journey. A 42-minute hop from Tampa to Atlanta? You'll spend more time watching the gate agent wrestle with the PA system than you will in the air. So, embrace the madness. Bring entertainment. Meditate. Write your memoirs. Or do what I do—people-watch and make notes for a book.

Because when it comes to air travel, the only thing that takes off on time...is your patience.

## Germ Sharing

**Thank you, because I'm tired of being healthy.** Yes, the air is filtered. But don't worry—germs are resourceful little buggers. They cling to tray tables, armrests, seat belts, and that mystery goo on the window shade. If it's been touched by 147 strangers and wiped once with a cocktail napkin, it's fair game.

To minimize your chances of becoming a walking science experiment:

- Avoid touching your face.
- Wash your hands like you're prepping for surgery.
- Wipe down your seat area like you're the last line of defense.

If you must cough, sneeze, or launch a monologue, please do so into your elbow. Bonus points if you make it dramatic.

Clean, clean, clean!

## Wearing a Mask

**Are you a superhero?** If you're feeling under the weather—or just want to avoid catching whatever's floating around—wearing a mask at the airport or on the plane is perfectly acceptable. In fact, it's considerate.

Yes, some folks still associate masks with COVID, but let's be honest: there are plenty of other reasons to mask up. Like the guy in 7B who's been crop-dusting the cabin since takeoff. Or the passenger behind you who packed a tuna sandwich and a side of armpit.

Truth is, I often wish I had a mask handy—not for health reasons, but for olfactory survival. So, if you're flying, wear a mask if you're sick—or if your seatmate is. Don't judge others who do. They might have a medical condition and are dodging germs... or just your Brussels sprout breath.

Flying is a shared experience. Let's all try to make it less a field of germs and pungency.

## Seatbelt Sign

**Oh, there's a sign?** What part of the seatbelt sign don't you understand? It's not even in a language—just a glowing little icon of a belt. Universal. Unambiguous. No excuse. And yes, the flight attendant explained it during the safety briefing (you did pay attention to that, didn't you?).

Yet somehow, there's always someone who doesn't listen, refuses to follow instructions, or pretends to buckle up. Is it rebellion? Laziness?

And then there's the one who decides to get up when the seatbelt sign is on. I suppose they're special. Perhaps they think turbulence is a myth, like Bigfoot or punctual baggage handlers.

Now, if you do have an emergency signal the attendant. Don't just leap up like you're storming the cockpit.

How about the click-happy folks who unbuckle the nanosecond the light goes off. I suggest keeping it on, just loosen it a bit. That way, if you doze off and the sign pops back on, you won't be jolted awake by a seatbelt scramble.

Wearing your seatbelt at all times keeps you secure in case of unexpected turbulence. Not wearing it can interfere with emergency evacuations.

So, buckle up. It's not just a rule—it's a courtesy.

# Blaming Agents for Delays/Cancellations

**It's not their fault!** Airline agents are not the reason your flight was delayed, canceled, rerouted through Cleveland, or mysteriously vanished. They didn't summon the thunderstorm. They didn't break the plane. They didn't personally overbook the flight because they hate your haircut. They are simply the unlucky souls chosen to stand between you and your vacation meltdown.

So, before you unleash your inner Hulk at the counter, the agent is not your enemy. They are your travel therapist and your gatekeeper to sanity.

Yelling at them is like blaming the waiter because the chef burned your steak. Or blaming the weatherperson because it's raining on your wedding. Or blaming your dog because your fantasy football team lost. Instead, be nice. Smile. Use words like "please" and "thank you." Offer them a snack. Compliment them. You'll be amazed how far charm goes.

And if you must vent, do it creatively. Write a haiku. Compose a limerick. Start a podcast. Just don't take it out on the agent—they're already one bad day away from becoming a cruise director.

## Blaming Pilots
## For Not Flying in Bad Weather

**How about some respect?** Let's stop blaming pilots when flights are delayed due to bad weather. They're not being overly cautious or lazy—they're doing their job, which is to get you safely from point A to point B without turning the trip into a white-knuckle thrill ride. These men and women are highly trained professionals who can fly through just about anything short of a volcanic eruption. But just because they can doesn't mean they should.

When the weather turns ugly—high winds, lightning, low visibility, or storms that make the radar look like a Jackson Pollock painting—the smart move is to wait it out. Some aircraft aren't built to handle those conditions, and even the ones that are have limits. Pushing those limits to keep a schedule isn't brave. It's reckless.

These decisions aren't made in isolation. Pilots, dispatchers, and flight operations teams work together, using real-time data and years of experience to decide whether it's safe to fly. If they say no, it's not because they're afraid of a little rain. It's because they're looking out for you—and everyone else on board.

So, the next time your flight's delayed, try not to roll your eyes or mutter about how "it doesn't look that bad out." You're not being inconvenienced—you're being protected. Don't blame the pilot. Don't blame the airline. In fact, don't blame anyone for putting your safety ahead of your schedule.

Instead, take a breath. Grab a snack. Maybe even thank the crew for making the tough call. After all, arriving late is annoying. Not arriving at all? That's a much bigger problem.

# Getting Up
# as Soon as the Plane Lands

**Let's go!** It happens every time. The wheels touch down, the cabin jolts slightly, and before the plane has even slowed to a crawl, there's a ding!—the seatbelt sign goes off—and suddenly it's like someone fired the starting pistol at the Aisle Olympics. Passengers spring to their feet like popcorn in a hot skillet, arms flailing, heads ducking, elbows jabbing, all in a frantic race to grab their overhead bags. It's a chaotic ballet of impatience, performed in a space barely wide enough for a beverage cart.

Why the rush? The door isn't open. The jet bridge isn't even in sight. We're still taxiing, people! You're not going anywhere for at least another 10 to 15 minutes.

And yet, there they stand—aisle blockers, bag wrestlers, and the occasional aisle squatter who decides now is the perfect time to check their phone, stretch, or reapply lip balm. Meanwhile, the rest of us sit quietly, seatbelts still fastened, watching this strange ritual unfold like it's part of the in-flight entertainment. It's not just impatience—it's performance art.

What if we all just stayed seated? What if we waited until the plane actually reached the gate, the door opened, and the rows ahead of us began to move? You'd still get off the plane at the same time, minus the awkward stand-and-wait routine and the risk of a carry-on bag to the face.

So, next time, resist the urge to leap up like your seat is on fire. Sit back. Relax. You've made it. The finish line isn't going anywhere—and neither are you—at least not for a while.

# Changing Diapers

**What's that smell?** There you are, minding your own business, when the unmistakable aroma of baby business wafts through the cabin. And wouldn't you know it—the source is right next to you Why couldn't this have been handled before boarding?

I get it. Babies don't operate on a schedule. But when the changing happens at the seat, mid-flight, it's not just unpleasant—it's unsanitary. The sights, the smells, the lingering souvenir diaper tucked into seatback full of, well, you know, is a full sensory assault.

Diaper changes belong in the restroom. Most planes have a changing table, or at least a toilet seat that can be lined with a disposable sanitary sheet. If you need help, flight attendants are trained professionals.

So, please, for the love of fresh air and public decency, take it to the bathroom. Your fellow passengers will thank you. And your baby? They'll still love you, even if you skip the seat-side spa treatment.

## Joking About the Pilot or Plane

**I just had five beers with the pilot!** Let's get one thing straight: joking that the pilot is drunk is not edgy, clever, or the next viral TikTok. It's just downright stupid! Saying "I just had five beers with the pilot" might earn you a few nervous chuckles—right before it earns you a one-way ticket to the no-fly list and a very awkward conversation with airport security.

Airlines don't have a "just kidding" department. They have protocols. And those protocols don't care if you were "just being funny." That little joke could delay the flight, ground the crew, and launch a full investigation. The pilot might be pulled from duty. The passengers will hate you.

And when they trace the comment back to you—and they always will—you could be banned from flying that airline, fined, or even prosecuted. All because you thought you were the next stand-up star.

If your joke involves alcohol, pilots, bombs, or anything that sounds like it belongs in a bad action movie, keep it to yourself. Because in the sky, your sense of humor better come with a seat-belt sign.

If you think that was funny, it's not going to fly.

# Ignoring Safety Instructions

**What do I do now?** Let's face it—airplane safety briefings are the most ignored live performance in the sky. The flight attendant is up there giving it their all, pointing dramatically at exits, miming seatbelt buckles, and demonstrating how to don a life vest. And what's the audience doing? Reading thrillers about plane crashes, dozing off like they've already reached their final destination, or whispering to their seatmate, "I've flown a lot—I know this stuff." Uh, yeah, they don't.

These are the same people who, in an actual emergency, will leap up, scream, and try to pry open the overhead bin to retrieve their emotional support pillow.

Meanwhile, the rest of us are trying to remember whether we're supposed to inflate the life vest before or after exiting the aircraft (It's after).

So, here's a thought: if you can't point to your nearest exit without doing a full 360-degree spin and a shrug, you're not allowed to panic. You must remain seated, calm, and quietly reflect on your life choices.

So, next time you fly, do yourself—and everyone else—a favor. Put the book down. Pocket the phone. Give the safety briefing the respect it deserves. It's not just theater—it's survival. Listen up, people. Or at least pretend to.

## Baggage Handlers

**My suitcase is not a bag of trash!** Baggage handlers at airports—what can I say? You've seen the videos, maybe even witnessed it firsthand: bags hurled like they insulted someone's mother. It's as if the handlers just had an argument with your luggage and decided to settle it with a body slam. Over the years, I've lost count of how many bags I've had damaged from this kind of rough treatment.

I'm told one reason for the tossing is time pressure. But really—if they took a few extra seconds to treat each bag with care, would the plane suddenly miss its slot and spiral into chaos?

And then there's the issue of theft. Cameras are everywhere in airports, yet somehow, you open your bag and find your headphones have vanished like a magician's rabbit. If that happens, report it immediately to the airline and the lost and found. File a claim with TSA and the police, and don't forget to check with your insurance company—some policies may cover the loss.

Always hang on to your baggage tags. They're not just paper souvenirs; they're your lifeline for tracking and making claims. And if you're traveling with anything fragile or important, such as meds and jewelry, pack it in your carry-on. It's the only way to ensure it doesn't end up in a game of airport dodgeball.

# Crowding the Luggage Carousel

**It's a free for all!** Welcome to the post-flight Hunger Games, otherwise known as crowding the luggage carousel. It's not just a retrieval zone—it's a psychological thriller. First comes the existential dread: will your bag be there, or did it take a detour to Nashville? The carousel spins, your heart races, and every black roller bag looks suspiciously like yours.

Some passengers bolt off the plane like it's a triathlon, elbowing their way to the belt—only to wait 30 minutes for the first bag to appear. Bravo, sprinters. Enjoy your front-row seat to nothing.

Meanwhile, modern luggage is a sea of sameness. If you didn't bedazzle your bag with neon tape, a flamingo ribbon, or a laminated photo of your dog, good luck. You'll be playing "Is That Mine?" for the next hour.

If you're traveling with others, fan out like a SWAT team. Cover the perimeter. Communicate. This is not amateur hour. And once your bag appears, and you've confirmed it's yours, grab it and retreat to a neutral zone. Do not linger. Do not block the view. Do not create a human dam.

Finally, never leave your retrieved bags unattended while you hunt for more. That's how bags get adopted by strangers or flagged by security.

The carousel may be chaotic, but with a little strategy and a lot of patience, you can survive the madness—and maybe even enjoy the show.

## Lost Luggage

**My stuff! It's gone!** If you've never lost your luggage while flying, you either don't travel much or you're incredibly lucky. I've had bags go missing for a day or two, and others disappear into the great unknown, never to be seen again. If this happens to you, don't panic—just act fast.

First, report the loss immediately at your airline's baggage claim office. If there isn't one, head to the ticket counter. Sometimes the bag is still in the airport or even on the plane. Other times, it's taken a scenic detour to another city. Airline reps can often locate it quickly, saving you time and stress later. If they do find it, you can usually request delivery to your home or hotel—one small silver lining.

Be sure to file a claim and stay in touch with the airline. Many carriers now offer online tracking. If your bag is truly lost, the airline is responsible for reimbursing you. But don't stop there—check your credit card benefits and homeowner's insurance too. You might be covered in more ways than you think.

I've learned to always pack essentials in my carry-on: medications, chargers, a change of clothes. One time, I accidentally packed my prescriptions in my checked bag. Naturally, that was the one that vanished forever. I had to scramble to a local pharmacy and get everything reordered. Lesson learned.

These days, many travelers are using Bluetooth or GPS trackers to locate their bags. It's oddly comforting to know your suitcase is enjoying a layover in Cleveland while you're stuck in Tampa.

Also, take a photo of your bag before you check it. It makes describing it to airline staff much easier—especially when you're trying to distinguish your black roller bag from the other 4,000 black roller bags on the planet.

And don't throw away your luggae tags, they contain personal encrypted data.

Finally, know your rights. Airlines have time limits for returning your luggage and may offer compensation for delays or expenses. But you'll need to ask—politely, persistently, and possibly with a touch of desperation.

# Sleeping With Your Feet in the Aisle

**Aaaah, this is better!** Stretching out, drifting off into slumberland and then—WHAM! Someone trips over your toes and spills their ginger ale.

Let's keep this simple: the aisle is not your ottoman. It's a narrow, high-traffic zone for passengers, carts, and flight attendants who are scanning faces, not scanning for stray feet. The last thing they need is to go airborne because your size 13s are staging a sneak attack.

Keep your legs, arms, and feet inside your designated space at all times. Sleeping with your feet in the aisle isn't just inconsiderate—it's a tripping hazard. Especially at night, when the cabin's dark and dreams are deep.

So, tuck 'em in, folks. This isn't your living room. It's a flying tube of shared space and limited patience.

## Blocking Aisles and Seats at the Gate

**Can I get through, please?** Ah, the airport gate area—where spatial awareness goes to die. What should be a simple waiting zone often transforms into a luggage labyrinth, a human game of Frogger, and a passive-aggressive seating showdown.

I'm consistently amazed by the creativity with which travelers deploy their bags. Some position them directly in front of their seats. Others place them on empty chairs, reserving space for their beloved carry-ons while people stand nearby, clutching boarding passes and dignity.

Then there are the floor campers—kids sprawled out mid-terminal, deep in a Lego battle or a snack-fueled nap, right where foot traffic flows. I get it, they need space. But maybe not the space where someone is trying to roll their suitcase without flattening a toddler.

To be fair, some gate areas are tighter than a middle seat on a budget airline. Still, there are ways to coexist without turning the terminal into a turf war. Try sliding your bag under your seat, placing it between your legs like a loyal pet, or tucking it nearby but not in the path of the next stampede to Zone 3.

And if your bag needs its own seat, it better have a boarding pass or a frequent flyer number

So, next time you're waiting to board, remember: it's not just about your comfort. It's about not turning the gate into a gladiator arena of rolling bags, blocked aisles, and territorial seat claims. Be kind. Be spatially aware. And for heaven's sake, don't make me hurdle your duffel bag to get to my seat.

# Asking to Be Upgraded For Free

**But I want to sit in first class!** So, you want to sit in first class without paying for it. Bold. Noble. Slightly delusional. But hey, we admire your spirit. Before you start practicing your "Don't you know who I am?" speech, let's review the unofficial, totally made-up, but surprisingly effective etiquette for scoring a free upgrade.

First, timing is everything. Try your luck on slow travel days—midweek flights or off-season routes. Avoid peak times unless you enjoy rejection with a side of eye-roll.

Second, be polite. This should go without saying, but alas, it must be said. Do not stomp up to the counter. Use your inside voice. Maybe even compliment their lanyard. Charm is your currency now.

Third, have a story. Are you flying to a wedding? A funeral? A wedding and a funeral? Mention it. Subtly. You're not auditioning for a soap opera, but a little heartfelt context never hurts.

Fourth, book smart. Sometimes booking early helps. Sometimes booking late helps. Sometimes nothing helps. It's basically airline roulette.

And finally, whether you end up in 1A or 32F next to a someone eating tuna salad with their fingers, thank the agent. They hold the keys to the kingdom—and the overhead bin space.

Remember: upgrades are like unicorns. Rare, magical, and more likely to appear if you don't act like you deserve one.

# Poking and Grabbing Flight Attendants

**Please, do not touch!** This isn't kindergarten, and flight attendants are not your personal snack dispensers. Poking, grabbing, tapping, or tugging at their uniforms is not only rude—it's downright inappropriate. Would you do this to a waiter? A nurse? A barista? If so, we need to talk.

Flight attendants are trained professionals who are constantly scanning the cabin, anticipating needs, and responding to requests. If you require something, use the call button. That's what it's there for. Then wait your turn, greet them with a smile, and ask politely. Revolutionary, I know.

Touching an attendant in any way—aside from a respectful handshake or a shoulder tap in a true emergency—is unacceptable. Depending on how aggressive you are, it may be a Federal offense and could result in fines, removal from the aircraft, or even criminal charges.

So, let's be perfectly clear: no poking, no grabbing, no tugging, no tapping, no pointing at your mouth like a baby bird. If you're tempted to reach out, reach inward instead. Reflect. Breathe. Then press the button like a civilized human being. Whatever you do, keep your hands off.

# Curbside Drop Off/Pick Up

**At least close your door!** The convenience of curbside drop-off and pick-up is wonderful—until you actually try it. Then it becomes a test of patience, reflexes, and your ability to suppress primal screams.

Outside most airports I've visited, the curb is pure chaos. There's rarely enough room to handle the flood of cars coming and going. Vehicles are often parked three deep, doors and trunks flung open, people lingering in long goodbyes while others try to squeeze in or out like a game of Tetris.

Sometimes, there's traffic control. They guide cars to open spots, make everyone wait for a clear path. It slows things down, sure—but at least there's a shred of order. Without it, it's every driver for themselves: squeezing in, blocking lanes, and pretending turn signals are optional.

Add a tight flight deadline, and the anxiety spikes. People loiter in the pick-up zone like they're waiting for a parade. You should only stop if your passenger is ready.

And please—if you're dropping someone off, say your goodbyes before you pull up. A quick hug or kiss is fine.

So, go early. Breathe deeply. Use your turn signal. And…close your door!

# Concessions

**I'll have the ten dollar Coke, please.** Have you bought snacks or food at an airport lately? Yeah— brace your wallet. That $4 granola bar? Now $8. The $2 bottle of water? Try $6. And don't even look directly at the pre-made sandwich unless you're ready to refinance your house. Why is everything so expensive? A few reasons.

First, rent is sky-high. Airport vendors pay premium leases for the privilege of selling you a $12 muffin. Second, supply logistics are a nightmare. Getting goods past security and into the terminal is a costly, time-consuming dance. Third, competition is limited. Once you're past TSA, it's a culinary monopoly. You're not choosing between options—you're choosing between hunger and bankruptcy. Fourth, airports take a cut of every sale, plus charge vendors for security and utilities. And finally, security restrictions mean you can't bring your own drinks, and some foods are frowned upon (see: "Airplane Food" and the Great Nut Ban of 2019).

Some airports are trying to rein in prices, but progress is slow. In the meantime, here's how to fight back. Bring your own snacks—TSA allows many food items through security. Just skip the nuts unless you want to trigger a cabin-wide panic. Carry an empty water bottle and fill it post-security to save $5. And if you're active duty, retired military, or simply in need, check with USO (United Serice Organization) or Traveler's Aid. These havens can offer comfort, snacks, and a break from the madness.

Airports: where time stands still, gates change without warning, and a small bag of trail mix costs more than your checked luggage. Bon appétit.

# Refusing to Put Bags Under the Seats

**I don't want it to get dirty!** I get it. You don't want your precious bag to touch the floor. It might get dirty. Heaven forbid it mingles with the common carpet. But here's the thing: that space under your seat? It's not yours. It's the legroom lifeline for the person behind you.

Airlines aren't asking for much. Big bags go in the overhead bin. Small bags—purse, backpack, laptop—go under the seat in front of you. It's not rocket science. It's not even tray-table science.

Yet I've sat next to people with bags so large they could double as studio apartments. They wedge them in anyway. Others refuse entirely, citing legroom, cleanliness, or some vague personal philosophy.

**Did you know:** A woman was forcefully kicked off a flight at a Chinese airport as she caused a one-hour delay after she refused to stow her Louis Vuitton purse under the seat.

The unidentified passenger was sitting in economy class seat in the flight that was ready to take off from an airport in Chongqing municipality.

But the aircraft was forced to return to the boarding gate after the flight crew requested the lady to keep her purse under the chair but kept being rebuffed. (Source: DailyMail.co.uk)

If your bag doesn't fit under the seat, it goes overhead. If it doesn't fit overhead, it gets checked. If it doesn't get checked, it becomes a safety hazard. And if it becomes a safety hazard, we all get delayed.

Turbulence doesn't care about your bag's feelings. It will launch that thing into the aisle like a rogue bowling ball. And when it does, your refusal to follow a simple rule becomes everyone's problem.

So, please. For the love of legroom, safety, and sanity—just put the bag where it belongs. Under the seat. Not beside it. Not between your knees. Not in the aisle. Not on your lap like a therapy animal. Under. The. Seat.

It's not a suggestion. It's a rule. And it's not about you. It's about all of us getting where we're going without tripping over your tote.

# Unruly Passengers

**Hey, you wanna fight?** Ah yes, the battle cry of the airborne barbarian. You've seen them before—those high-strung gladiators of the sky who treat every minor inconvenience like a personal insult. Their coffee's lukewarm? Outrage. Their seat doesn't recline? Betrayal. Their neighbor dares to breathe audibly? Time to square up.

These folks don't just argue—they perform. They spar with servers, duel with coworkers, feud with neighbors, and when they board a plane, they bring their full Broadway production of "I'm Always Right: The Musical."

Fortunately, flight crews are trained in the ancient art of passenger pacification. They use subtle code words like "Mr. Sunshine in 14B" or "We've got a spicy meatball in Row 22" to alert each other.

**Did you know:** Federal law prohibits interfering with aircraft crew or physically assaulting or threatening to physically assault aircraft crew or anyone else on an aircraft. Passengers are subject to civil penalties for such misconduct, which can threaten the safety of the flight by disrupting or distracting cabin crew from their safety duties. Additionally, federal law provides for criminal fines and imprisonment of passengers who interfere with the performance of a crewmember's duties by assaulting or intimidating that crewmember. (Source: FAA.gov)

If you find yourself seated next to one of these airborne agitators, do not engage. Do not make eye contact. Do not offer snacks. Simply press the call button and whisper, "We've got a live one." The crew will know what to do. They've dealt with worse—like the woman who insisted her emotional support ferret needed a window seat.

# Cabin Cleanliness

**Was there a party in here?** Most airlines do their best to clean the cabin after each flight. However, as I'm sure you've experienced—especially when your elbow sticks to the tray table—the results aren't always sparkling. Some airlines employ dedicated cleaning crews, while others rely on flight attendants to tidy up between flights. Given the constraints of staffing, time, and the general wear and tear of the cabin, a thorough cleaning isn't always possible.

**Did you know:** Thanks to HEPA filters and efficient circulation on commercial aircrafts, the air you breathe in flight—though not necessarily entirely virus-free—is much cleaner than the air in restaurants, bars, stores, or your best friend's living room. Here's why you don't need to fear the air up there.(Source: NationalGeographic.com)

There are three types of cleaning procedures. The deep clean is the most thorough and usually happens overnight. The overnight clean is second-best. And then the turn clean, which is a quick once-over during a fast turnaround—it's like a "lick and a promise" version of cabin hygiene.

The areas of most concern include tray tables, screens, carpets, armrests, seats, overhead bins, door handles, seat pockets, call buttons, air nozzles (those little "eyeballs"), buckles, and bathrooms. The cleaning process is intensive and time-consuming, and despite best efforts, you may still find a mystery wrapper or a half-read romance novel tucked into the seat pocket.

You can help by washing your hands and cleaning up after yourself. It's a small gesture, but it helps. And if you're a stickler for cleanliness, book an early morning flight—those are most likely to be the cleanest, thanks to the overnight deep clean that happens while the rest of us are dreaming of legroom.

# Overbooking

**But wait. I have a ticket!** You've planned your trip with military precision. You've packed, prepped, and even remembered your neck pillow. You arrive at the gate, ticket in hand, ready to board—and then the gate agent smiles and says, "We're sorry, this flight is overbooked."

Wait. What? OVERBOOKED? I HAVE A TICKET! Yes, you do. But in airline-speak, a ticket is more of a polite suggestion than a promise. Airlines routinely sell more seats than they have, like a restaurant taking reservations for tables that don't exist. It's not a glitch—it's a strategy based on collected data.

They assume some passengers won't show up, and they want every seat filled. It's like planning a dinner party for eight, inviting twelve, and hoping four choke on their appetizers.

Buried deep in the ticket terms—right after "non-refundable" and just before "we own your luggage now"—is a clause that says you may be denied boarding due to overbooking. Translation: "We sold your seat twice. Good luck!"

Before they boot you off involuntarily, airlines must first ask for volunteers. This is where things get theatrical. A gate agent announces, "We're offering a $200 voucher and a seat on the next flight!" Cue the stampede of bargain hunters and travel gamblers. If no one bites, the offer goes up. $400. $600. Eventually someone caves.

Yes, airlines are required to offer something in return. But what you get depends on how much you complain. Be polite but firm. And if you're involuntarily bumped, know your rights. Ask for written documentation. Ask for compensation. Ask for snacks. You've earned it.

Check in early. The early bird gets the seat. The late bird gets a voucher and a sandwich. Join the frequent flyer program—loyalty might save your butt. Avoid peak travel times. Fewer people means fewer chances of being left hanging. And for heaven's sake, don't wear flip-flops. You want to look like someone who deserves a seat.

Meanwhile, lurking in the terminal are the ticket scavengers—those brave souls hoping to snag a cheap seat from a no-show. They hover like vultures over a buffet, ready to pounce. It's a risky game, but for them, overbooking is a lifestyle.

So, yes, you have a ticket. But until you're in the seat and the plane is taxiing, you're just a contestant in the great airline lottery.

Smile, nod, and pray you're not the one holding the musical chair when the music stops.

# Asking Stupid Questions

**Where is the nearest electrical outlet?** Some say the only stupid question is the one not asked. But those people have clearly never worked at an airport. Because once you've heard "Can I open a window for some fresh air?" at 35,000 feet, you start to believe that maybe—just maybe—some questions should stay unasked, unspoken, and ideally, unthought.

Airports and airplanes are magnets for the marvelously misinformed. There's always that one traveler who stands directly beneath a glowing "Gate B12" sign and asks, "Is this Gate B12?" Or the guy frantically waving down a gate agent to ask, "Is this the flight to Chicago?"—while holding a boarding pass that says Phoenix. Then there's the classic: "Where's the nearest electrical outlet?" usually asked while leaning against one, phone in hand, battery at 2%, and panic at 98%.

Onboard, the hits keep coming. "What's in the BLT sandwich?" or "Where are the safety instructions?"

"What time is it?" is a fan favorite—especially when asked mid-flight, mid-nap, mid-time zone. And "When do we land?" is often delivered with the urgency of someone who just realized they left the oven on in 1997.

Flight attendants, bless them, deserve medals, massages, and maybe a mute button. They've fielded questions like "Can I use the bathroom while we're landing?" (Sure, if you enjoy turbulence and regret.) Or "Can I switch seats with the pilot?" (Only if you brought your own license and a strong sense of irony.)

And let's not forget the parking lot philosophers: "How do I get to the cell phone lot?"—usually asked of someone who is clearly a fellow traveler, wearing Crocs and dragging a suitcase with one wheel. It's a miracle we ever make it to our destinations.

So, yes, ask questions. But maybe—just maybe—read the signs, check the seatback pocket, and resist the urge to ask if the plane has Wi-Fi after you've been streaming Netflix for an hour.

## The Clothes People Wear

**What are you wearing?** Now, I'm certainly no fashion police. I dress simply every day—nothing flashy, just a decent shirt, pants, and shoes (Adidas, to be sure). But I do try to be presentable when I'm out in public.

Airports, though? They've become the new front row of the fashion free-for-all.

From pajama bottoms and fuzzy slippers to spandex that leaves nothing to the imagination, from bare feet padding through security to outfits that seem better suited for a nightclub—or a nap—it's a parade of "Did I just see that?"

I get it. Travel is stressful. Comfort matters. But somewhere along the way, we traded "travel attire" for "couch couture." And while I'm not here to dictate your wardrobe, I will say this: maybe—just maybe—think twice before stepping out in something that might make fellow travelers avert their eyes or question your grasp on zippers.

Airports, restaurants, grocery stores—anywhere the public gathers—deserve a little respect. You don't need to dress to the nines. Just aim for "not embarrassing."

There are some things we just don't want to see.

## Personal Pillows

**Are those stains on that pillow case?** There's a special breed of traveler who boards the plane not with a neck pillow or a discreet travel cushion, but with a full-blown, queen-sized, memory-foam pillow—complete with a pillowcase that looks like it's been through a breakup, a barbecue, and a bachelor party. It's clutched like a security blanket, dragged down the aisle like Linus from Peanuts, and then—brace yourself—pressed against the airplane wall.

Let's talk about that wall. It's not just a structural feature—it's a microbial mural. It's been sneezed on, coughed at, leaned against, and possibly licked by a toddler mid-tantrum. And now your pillow is absorbing all of it like a sponge.

Meanwhile, the pillowcase itself often tells a story: a faint yellow halo from hair gel, a mysterious blotch shaped like Idaho, or a crusty corner. If your pillowcase has more personality than your passport photo, it's time for a little self-reflection—and a hot wash.

Even if your pillow has only been used "a couple times," it may already carry the aromatic bouquet of dry shampoo, scalp oils, and last night's dreams. And please, don't wedge it between the seat and the fuselage like you're building a pillow fort. That's not insulation—it's contamination.

If you must bring a pillow on board, make it a dedicated travel pillow. One that's compact, machine-washable, and doesn't double as your Netflix-and-chill companion at home. Bonus points if it comes with a fresh, crisp cover that doesn't scream "I slept on this during a fever dream."

## Photos On Your Phone

**Wait. What is that?** Let's talk about a new in-flight entertainment trend: scrolling through your phone's photo library for the entire flight. No headphones, no movie, just a personal slideshow of your life—on full display for your seatmates.

Now, I'm not naming names (and please don't use me as an example!), but this has happened to me three times recently. Three! Both men and women. I'm minding my own business, trying to read or nap, and suddenly I'm an unwilling co-pilot on someone's photographic journey through birthdays, beach trips, blurry screenshots, and— oh dear—photos that should never be viewed in public, let alone in a middle seat with strangers on either side.

I try not to look. I really do. But when someone's phone is six inches from your face, it's hard not to catch a glimpse. And let me tell you, some of those glimpses cannot be unseen.

So, here's a friendly reminder: If you're going to scroll through your photos on a plane, maybe do a little pre-flight cleanup. Or at least tilt your screen away from your innocent seatmates.

And hey…what was that last photo you were looking at?

# Cell Phone Waiting Lots

**I think I'll just wait right here...** Said every oblivious driver ever, as they pulled into the breakdown lane. Never mind the signs, the traffic, or the fact that they're now one hazard cone away from starring in a highway safety video.

Meanwhile, the rest of us are doing what responsible, law-abiding, non-menace-to-society citizens do: waiting in the cell phone lot. You know, that magical place with actual parking spaces, no honking, and zero chance of being rear-ended by a shuttle bus.

Cell phone waiting lots are a gift—an oasis of order in the chaos of airport pickups. You can sit there, sip your coffee, check your texts, and wait for the "I'm here!" message without risking a citation.

Yet somehow, every time I go to the airport, I witness the same parade of shoulder squatters. Cars idling in no-parking zones like they're in a drive-thru. Hazard lights blinking like, "It's fine, I'm invisible!"

So, if you're picking someone up, use the cell phone lot. It's free. It's safe. It doesn't make you the villain in someone else's travel story. Don't be that person who turns a simple pickup into a traffic jam with a side of road rage.

# Riding the Tram

**Let the games begin!** Some of the larger airports provide trams to shuttle you from the parking lot to the terminal—or even between terminals. While the ride itself is usually uneventful, it's the getting on and off that delivers the real excitement.

For reasons unknown to civilized society, when those doors open, people rush like they're fleeing a wild beast. I was once standing directly in front of the doors, waiting to board, and as soon as they opened, a hoard of crazed travelers surged past me like I was frozen in time. By the time the dust settled, the tram was full—and I was still standing there, blinking in disbelief.

I see this more and more wherever entrance lines form. What compels people to disregard everyone around them just to be first inside? My upbringing taught me to let others go first—especially women and children—but too many men don't follow the same courtesy rules I do. So, I'm often left behind, watching the stampede from the sidelines.

The same goes for seating. I'll stand so others can sit. Some people say "thank you," but most don't. It's as if basic manners have been replaced by a race to nowhere.

Well, I've learned my lesson. I now prepare for the tram battle like a seasoned warrior. I position myself next to the door for a quick exit—and maybe, just maybe, a fighting chance to board.

## Flight Attendants

**Thank you!** Flying isn't just about getting from Point A to Point B—it's a floating social experiment. And while passengers are busy jockeying for overhead bin space and elbow room, flight attendants are juggling safety, service, and sanity.

Board with a smile. You don't have to curtsy, but a warm "hello" as you step onboard sets the tone. Flight attendants see hundreds of faces a day—make yours one that radiates respect.

A granola bar, chocolate, or other tiny offerings aren't bribes—they're morale boosters. You'd be amazed how far a little treat goes in a pressurized cabin.

Mind Your Manners: "Please" and "thank you" aren't just for kindergarten. They're the currency of civility. Use them liberally, especially when asking for that third soda.

As you deplane, toss out a sincere "Thanks for the great flight!" It's the verbal mint on the pillow. And yes, they remember it.

## Tossing the Bags

**That's okay—just toss my bag like a bag of trash! Geez!** Why is it that baggage check-in agents and handlers toss our bags like they're dead meat? Would it kill them to show a little consideration and gently lay the bag on the belt?

We're told to limit the weight of our bags so they can be handled without strain. But judging by the way they're flung around, maybe we should raise the weight limit—give them something to think twice about!

It's no wonder nice bags come through the turnstile looking like they've survived a bar fight. I've learned to pack anything fragile dead-center in my suitcase, surrounded by layers of clothing, like a protective cocoon against bag torture.

Hard-shell cases—those "dent-proof" wonders—are gaining popularity, and it's no mystery why. They're not just luggage anymore; they're armor.

I've actually said "thank you" to someone who treated my bag with care. That shouldn't be necessary, but it's so rare, I feel compelled to acknowledge the kindness. It's like spotting a unicorn in the wild.

# Walking Through the Airport

**A point for everyone you hit. Let's go!!** Sounds simple, right? There you are, in a massive airport, and suddenly it feels like you've been dropped into a game of human dodgeball.

People are everywhere—distracted, determined, or downright dangerous. Some are glued to their phones, others scanning the ceiling like it holds the secrets of their gate assignment, and a few are in such a hurry they'll mow down anything in their path.

Then there's the "wall walkers"—four or five people wide, strolling side by side like they're leading a parade, making zero effort to let anyone pass.

My personal favorite? The group that plants themselves smack in the middle of the walkway to discuss dinner plans or debate what they'll do first when they arrive. Because clearly, the best place for a roundtable is the busiest corridor in the terminal.

And let's not forget the moving sidewalks. Some folks treat them like a ride at Universal—step on, stand still, and stare at their phones as if the rest of us don't exist.

If you've read my other *Crazy!* books, you know I'm a student of human behavior. I'm always watching, always anticipating: who's going to do what, when, where, and how. The "why"? That's a mystery for another day.

And so, I work my way through the airport as if I am driving a car with a newborn strapped in their car seat. Glide, don't collide. Thank you.

## Is There a Line Here?

**That's okay—go ahead and butt in front of me!** Apparently, waiting lines these days are just a suggestion. Choose your own adventure: stand wherever you like, maybe even start a new line off to the side.

I see it everywhere—buffets, theater entrances, ticket counters, restaurants, and most maddeningly, merging lanes on the highway. It's as if the concept of "waiting your turn" has been replaced by "whoever's boldest wins."

Can you imagine Disney World without the velvet ropes? Chaos would reign. Mickey would need a whistle and riot gear.

And the same folks who cut the line are often the first to scold someone else for doing the same. Hypocrisy with a side of entitlement.

Please—just get in the back of the line. Wait your turn. Is shaving off two minutes really worth the stink eye from everyone else?

# Superstitions

**"Good luck!?** There are many passengers and crewmembers who have strong feelings about rituals and superstitions.

Here are just a few of the things people do when flying:

- Avoiding flying on Friday the 13th (or any Friday) and sitting in row 13.
- Touching or kissing the outside of the aircraft when boarding the plane.
- Wearing, or carrying, a good luck charm.
- Listening to a particular song or reciting a special saying during takeoff and landing.
- Making the Sign of the Cross before takeoff or landing.
- Holding hands with the person next to you.
- Wearing the same clothes for each flight.
- Wearing socks inside out.
- Sending a photo of the plane to a loved one.
- Doing a short dance upon entering the aircraft.
- Holding a stuffed animal during the flight.

If you see any of these things on your next flight, understand that someone may be trying to feel okay in a stressful moment.

Now where did I put that lucky charm...?

# Tips for Courteous and Friendly Flying

To summarize everything you have read, here is a checklist of things to consider when flying:

### For Safety (Yours and Everyone's)

- Remove headphones for the safety briefing, even if you've heard it before.
- Keep your seatbelt fastened throughout the flight.
- Locate the exits and take note of who's around you in case of emergency.
- Place carry-ons under the seat in front of you; keep aisles clear.
- Clean hands help keep everyone healthier.
- Be willing to help if asked.

### For Courtesy and Comfort

- Wait your turn—no elbowing!
- A simple "thank you" to the crew goes a long way.
- Snack cart etiquette: Remove headphones, lower your tray, and assist with passing items.
- Respect those trying to sleep or relax.
- A pre-flight shower is a gift to your seatmates.

- Use headphones: No one wants to hear your movie or music.
- Hand over trash or take it with you.
- Drink water, not just wine.
- Don't linger in the bathrooms—others are waiting.

### For Shared Space Harmony

- Check behind you before leaning back.
- Share the seat space—no elbow wars.
- Keep tabs on kids and pets.
- Shoes stay on: Especially if your socks are expressive.
- Help with bags or seating if someone's struggling.

### For Extra Kindness

- Write a thank-you note: A kind word to the crew or airline can brighten their day.
- Be nice: Always the best travel accessory.

Thank you. Enjoy your next flight!

# Afterword

I hope you enjoyed flying with me and learning about the many inappropriate, inconsiderate, dangerous, and irresponsible behaviors and situations encountered at the airport and on the plane.

Hopefully, after reading this book, you'll be more aware of these things, how to avoid doing them, and what you should do to when you encounter them.

Familiarize yourself with the airline rules and regulations. And take a moment to thank the pilots and crew members for your pleasant flight. They deserve it.

I hope you have enjoyed this book and I look forward to seeing you at the airport!

And when I see you on the plane, thank you for not . . .

- Reclining your seat into my lap without warning
- Hogging the armrests like you're claiming territory
- Playing your music or videos out loud (headphones, please!)
- Bringing a tuna sandwich onboard and unleashing it mid-flight

- Standing in the aisle during boarding like it's a cocktail party
- Treating the lavatory like your personal spa
- Ignoring the seatbelt sign because "you know better"
- Using the overhead bin like a game of Tetris with no winners
- Sneezing into the air like it's confetti
- Arguing with the crew—they're not your therapist or referee
- And for not...

**Flying Me Crazy!**

# About the Author

John Reinhardt has been designing books for 50 years with thousands of books to his credit. This is his fourth book as an author.

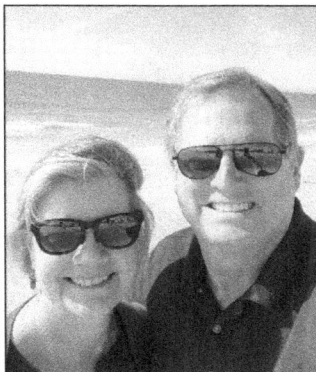

John lives in a wonderful golf community in central Florida with his wife, Lynn.

When he is not designing or writing books, he spends his time playing golf, traveling, gardening, brewing, creating things, getting together with friends, playing guitar, and just about anything else there is to do.

You can contact John at:
DesignerofBooks@gmail.com

For updates and information:
**www.YoureDrivingMeCrazy.com**

# If you enjoyed this book, you'll also want to read...

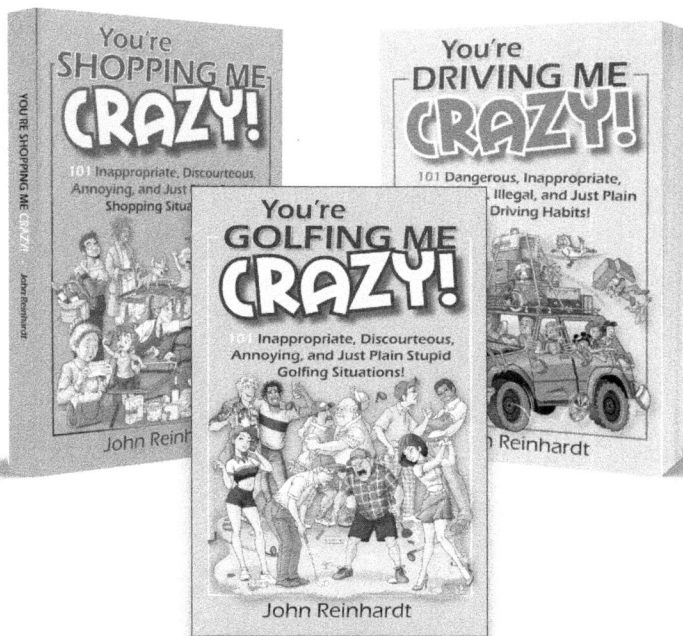

## More books coming soon!

### Available on Amazon and online bookstores!

youredrivingmecrazy.com